Aunties

Also by Tamara Traeder:

girlfriends: Invisible Bonds, Enduring Ties
(with Carmen Renee Berry,
Wildcat Canyon Press, 1995)

The girlfriends Keepsake Book:
The Story of Our Friendship
(with Carmen Renee Berry,
Wildcat Canyon Press, 1996)

girlfriends Talk About Men:
Sharing Secrets for a Great Relationship
(with Carmen Renee Berry,
Wildcat Canyon Press, 1997)

Edited by Julienne Bennett:

Where the Heart Is: A Celebration of Home
(with Mimi Luebbermann,
Wildcat Canyon Press, 1995)

Aunties

Our Older, Cooler, Wiser Friends

TAMARA TRAEDER
AND JULIENNE BENNETT

WILDCAT CANYON PRESS
A Division of Circulus Publishing Group, Inc.
Berkeley, California

Aunties: Our Older, Cooler, Wiser Friends

Editor: Roy M. Carlisle
Copyeditor: Mimi Kusch
Cover and Interior Design: Gordon Chun Design
Typesetting: Holly A. Taines
Typographic Specifications: Body text set in New Baskerville
10.5/17. Headers are Novarese Medium and Dorchester
Script.

Printed in the United States of America

Library of Congress Cataloging-in-Publication Data
Traeder, Tamara, 1960–
      Aunties : our older, cooler, wiser friends / Tamara
Traeder and Julienne Bennett.
      p. cm.
ISBN 1-885171-22-6 (pbk. : alk. paper)
1. Aunts. I. Bennett, Julienne, 1954–   . II. Title.
HQ759.94.T7   1998
306.87—dc21   98-11873   CIP

Distributed to the trade by Publishers Group West
10 9 8 7 6 5 4 3 2

To our nieces and nephews:
Jason, Tara, Paige, Molly, Emily, Amy, Katie,
and Sydney; and our aunties: Milly, Ági, and Dori;
and the memory of Connie and Marion

Contents

Acknowledgments

$\mathscr{M}$any thanks to all the incredible women who contributed their stories and enthusiasm to this project. We were honored to hear their stories, and were gratified by their warm response to the subject matter. Without their honesty and willingness to take time with us, there would be no book.

Tamara wishes to acknowledge the importance of Jason, Tara, and Paige in her life and to thank Terry and Glori Traeder for their support of her relationship with their children. She would also like to express her gratitude for Milly Cory and Connie Nesbitt, two women who greatly influenced her, and as always, for the continuing support of her parents, Gus and Fern Traeder, and good friend, Laura Rafaty.

Julienne is grateful for her nieces Molly and Emily Bennett who teach her first hand about the extraordinary bonds between aunties and nieces, and for Byron and Cheryl Bennett for their love and support. Bountiful thanks to Terry Griffin for his love, good humor, and patience as this book unfolded, to her mother, Irene Fencil, for always being there, and to Ági Ashley, her honorary auntie.

Hats off to Roy M. Carlisle for his brilliant editorial

guidance and friendship; Holly A. Taines for her hard work, long hours, and sense of humor; Leyza Yardley for her incredible organizational skills; and Rose Bargmann and Aimee Panyard for their verve and marketing acumen. Once again we thank the team at Gordon Chun Design for their unique and professional work. To Karen Cross, Kim Wylie, Kevin Votel, and the entire gang at Publishers Group West, thanks for believing in us.

Special thanks to Jill Sundberg for providing us with the original concept for this book and for sharing her stories.

Author's Note

We have changed some individuals' names and disguised certain characteristics in order to protect contributors' privacy.

Aunt Daisy

After you were gone I realized that you were precious,
that in the world of aunts I would not have another,
and especially not a Daisy, who so loved me,
that I would not hear a boatlike car turn in on the gravel
of the driveway, and see you smiling, heavy and plain
in your flowered dress, or hear your wavering voice
tell about the days when the aunts and uncles were young,
and I understood that in the great grand scheme of things,
of galaxies and molecules and the vast, expanding universe,
something irreplaceable had gone out of my life,
and not dreams, and not the spirit, and not the future world
would bring you back as you were again.

—Carolyn Miller

Where Would We Be without Our Aunties?

—PATRICIA MEYER SPACKS, *The Female Imagination*

*C*hildren are at risk. We are bombarded every day with news of young people taking weapons to school, sidetracking their lives with drugs, and suffering from the ill effects of divorce and teenage pregnancy. We hear the staggering statistic that the number of children in poverty is one in five. We know that even in middle-class homes well out of the poverty range, a child is more likely to be a "latchkey kid" or to have only one parent around as primary caretaker, a big change from the time when each child had two parents to watch over him or her.

Further, more and more parents are required to be fully employed outside the home to make ends meet. Unsupervised (or undersupervised) and isolated, children may regard themselves as unimportant, and develop a sense of low self-esteem, which may affect them for the rest of their lives. Worse, they may take dangerous risks in order to find a place to belong, a place which may ultimately destroy them. As Hillary

Rodham Clinton summarizes in her book *It Takes a Village,* "Everywhere we look, children are under assault: from violence and neglect, from the breakup of families, from the temptations of alcohol, tobacco, sex, and drug abuse, from greed, materialism, and spiritual emptiness. These problems are not new, but in our time they have skyrocketed."[1]

In this country, there have always been homes with two working parents, as well as single parent households. We do not believe that mothers choosing to enter the workplace, either out of necessity or desire, have caused this crisis for children. A mother who is doing what is necessary for her children's survival seems preferable to one who does not. A mother who has a sense of fulfillment and satisfaction from her work outside the home seems preferable to one who lives out her heart's desires through her children. The real difference is that working mothers and fathers no longer have the community of people—an extended family and trustworthy neighbors—to rely on to share child-rearing tasks. In the past, as this country spread into new territories and borders were extended, neighbors relied on each other for their very survival, and family members tended to stay in close physical proximity to each other. Things are different now, and families are more spread out. There is probably no one reading this book who doesn't have at least one family member who lives hundreds, if not thousands, of miles away.

Perhaps this physical separation from our families stems from our American heritage—a belief that a new home away from our birthplace will be better and fulfill our dreams. We move to a new place, as our ancestors did before us. Or perhaps the separation stems from a belief that separation from one's parents is necessary to avoid the mistakes that they made. As Dr. Mary Pipher points out in her book *The Shelter of Each Other,* maybe our zeal to protect children (and ourselves) from the interference of parents or other relatives has resulted in everyone's isolation: "Even twenty years ago, a common task was to help young families form strong boundaries between themselves and their extended kin. This was a time when parents-in-law were likely to live nearby and to want Sunday dinners together every week, when grandparents gave grandchildren too much candy and interfered with parental discipline and when many families had 'clothesline police' to check on when they were doing their laundry. Therapists helped these young families push back overinvolved relatives and make space and time for their new families. They helped couples set firm boundaries between themselves and their often intrusive parents. But while young families used to be overwhelmed by family, today young families often have no time with extended family. No one in the extended family knows their children or gives them anything. Young families often need to be connected, not distanced, from whatever family resources are available."[2] The dangers a child faces, mixed with the reality that individuals tend to be further apart physically from their own extended families, result in parents finding that they have few places to turn for assistance in their children's safe upbringing.

Of course, no parent wants to expose his or her children to a grandparent or other relative who is abusive, but the fact is, children need a lot of attention and love in order to survive to adulthood, and to be functional, caring, and responsible adults. As Dr. Evelyn Bassoff discusses in her book, *Cherishing Our Daughters,* even with two loving parents in their lives, children benefit from the love of many people. "How much happier our American children would be if they, too, know from the start that when mommy or daddy was busy or out of sorts, there were other arms to hold them, other ears to listen to them, and other laps to provide them safe refuge. And how much more relaxed we parents would be knowing we could count on loving support as we raised our children. The African proverb 'It takes an entire village to raise a child' is catching on in the United States, where men and women are learning firsthand that child rearing requires many hands and hearts and that it is permissible to reach outside the immediate family for help and guidance."[3]

So where do we turn? Every parent wants the best for his or her children, and there are few people who would argue that children thrive on isolation. Yet even "intact" families are less and less likely to spend their days together, each family member focused on commuting, keeping their jobs, or staying in school and other activities, all of which draw each of us away from one another. Not many parents and children work together side by side on the farm or in a family business, where they would have the opportunity to see each other and notice each other's reactions or moods, or have the luxury of a few spare moments together where parent and child can share how they are feeling or what is on their minds. As Ms. Clinton points out, "American mothers, both those who stay at home and those who work outside it, spend less than half an hour a day, on average, talking with or reading to their children, and fathers spend less than fifteen minutes."[4] That leaves a lot of time for a child to worry, alone with his or her problems, to become bored and fall into the passive activity of watching television, and to get into trouble. The whittling down of parents' opportunity to hear their children, however, does not diminish the need of those children to be heard. Children, and their frequently beleaguered and isolated parents, need help.

Aunties to the Rescue

We have an enormous resource in raising our children—each other. And among those who are chosen, or who offer themselves for the good of the children in their lives are aunties, women who, blood-related or not, step in and fill the need of children to be listened to, played with, comforted and loved. When parents recognize that they cannot handle it all, they frequently turn to a sibling or a close friend for help. Many times this is a woman, who becomes an auntie and part of the extended family. Sometimes those parents are aware of the need before a child is born, and go searching for an auntie who will help guide a child and keep him or her safe.

Other women see a child who needs some focused attention, care, or just more fun, and makes herself available for service in that child's life. Such is the case with Chris, a marketing manager in her twenties, whom we interviewed: "I have been an aunt since I was fourteen. My sister's first child was a boy, then she gave me two nieces after that.

"When the youngest one was around four, my sister got divorced. I had just finished college and had gotten a job, but I needed a place to live. She had no resources, so we all moved in together. We didn't live together for all that long, but my relationship with those kids started then. It just made sense to me that I step in then. I thought my sister did a good job, but I didn't want what happened to her to badly affect them. I didn't want them to have to struggle more than necessary. It seemed to me that they were the priority. Now in adulthood I love having made that decision."

Other Mothers

Many ethnic communities already know that auntie relationships are crucial in raising children, as described by Joan K. Peters, in her book *When Mothers*

Work. "The sociologist Patricia Hill Collins coined the term 'othermothers' to describe the network of 'grandmothers, sisters, aunts, or cousins who help raise other people's children. And when needed temporary child care arrangements can turn into long term care or informal adoption.' She refers to African American mothers, who not only have a history of communal child-rearing but whose community networks helped them to raise their children while they labored to put food on the table. . . . In her words, 'African American communities have also recognized that vesting one person with full responsibility for mothering a child many not be wise or possible.'

"This is also true, she notes, of Latina mothers, among whom a *co-madre*, or godmother, is responsible for certain aspects of child-rearing and has official baptismal functions. . . . The black family is also characterized by the open and flexible boundaries necessary for parent networks to function. According to Kenneth Hardy, chairman of the Department of Child and Family at Syracuse University, it is precisely this kind of family flexibility that allows 'for informal adoptions, surrogacy, and para-parenting.'

"The sociologist Pepper Schwartz finds that 'para-parenting' is now becoming a universal American phenomenon because one-quarter of American children live with one parent and one-quarter of the adult population lives alone. She describes a sort of committed, nonblood 'othermother' relationship that is becoming more common in this time of fragmented families. In other words, of necessity—as in the black community—the white community is finally learning the advantage of opening the family to community support, dispersing the mothering, and sharing parenting with others."[5]

Of course, sharing responsibilities of parenthood with others requires that parents allow another adult to have influence on a child and to develop a relationship separate from that between parent and child. A mother especially may feel guilt about this, as our culture encourages her to believe that she is to "be all" and know all about her child. Additionally, a parent may feel jealousy, envy, or fear if he or she sees a child developing a close relationship with another adult.

But children need other ears to listen to them, and other eyes to watch them. As Ms. Peters found, "The psychologist Sandra Scarr wrote an award-winning book in 1984 based on her extensive research showing that children benefit by learning to trust several adults rather than one."[6] It seems easy to believe that children benefit by more love rather than less. Most parents know this and try to act on it, even if it is at first difficult for them. As Ms. Peters cites, "NYU's Linda Carter offers the most important idea underlying the parenting network: a child's love is not a matter of competition. She says, 'The more love there is, the more the child's capacity for love grows. A child's loving relationship with a caregiver will mean more love—not less—for everyone.'"[7]

Dr. Bassoff encourages new parents to adopt this belief and to include more adults in their children's worlds, although conflicting feelings may arise: "It is perfectly natural for children of all ages to confide in, look up to, emulate, and even develop crushes on the special people who take an interest in them. For some parents, however, this sort of adoration can create feelings of exclusion, jealousy, or envy. . . . When clients tell me that they resent a special person in their daughter's life, I usually say something like this: 'Jealousy and envy are normal human feelings. They don't indicate that you are a bad person or a bad parent. Still, try to gather up all your courage and all your will not to *act* on these feelings lest they harm the child you love.'" Dr. Bassoff reports that she usually finds that, "committed to serving their child's best interest, most parents are willing to follow this advice."[8]

Children need "othermothers" and thrive with their attention, even if parents have to control some negative feelings about another adult in their lives. But many parents, and mothers in particular, are thrilled to have the help. As we shall see, parents may turn to a sibling, usually a sister, even one who is far away, to form a relationship with a child. Similarly, women's friendships often spawn an auntie relationship when one of the women has a child. In both cases, a parent has a person they trust, who understands the parents' own values and respects the parent/child relationship, taking the time and making the commitment to be there for that child. The parents, by reaching out to these women, create an extended family for their child, one of their own choosing, and provide another safe place for a child to learn and to be safe.

This is not to say that there are no men who care for children, or who are willing to step in when needed. Perhaps it is the traditional role of women as caretakers which causes us to look to the women in our circle to help raise our children. Whatever the case, we found from the people we interviewed that they looked to the women around them, blood-related or not, to help form their idea of "family." They stressed that their aunties, along with their mothers, were the ones who carried on their individual family traditions and values, who helped them define themselves as part of a family. Wendy, a fifty-four-year-old marketing director, described what she thought the role of an aunt is in the family: "I think kinship, the stories about who you are and where your family came from and the stories families tell themselves about who they are, are passed along by the women in the family. I think that's a function that aunts serve."

Olivia, a writer in her forties, recalls, "My aunt and my mother and I would quilt, and while we quilted we sang together. My aunt's family and our family were together on all the holidays, even holidays we invented, like progressive dinners we shared. It was always my mother and Aunt Anne putting these things together. It is hard to imagine not having my aunt there. My mom and aunt just stretched this love out and created a safe circle in which to be a woman. I remember my mother once telling me that I came from good stock. I know that shaped me."

When we look back over our lives to the people who most influenced us, many of us immediately think of our parents, a creative or inspired teacher who took an interest in us, or a hero we admired from afar. But if we think a little harder, we may find that we were shaped by another less obvious source—our aunties. We don't often hear about the importance of these relationships. We, the authors, hoped to get a glimpse of the intricacies and attributes of these auntie connections by interviewing dozens of women about the meaning of their relationships with their own aunties, and how they, in turn, viewed their own role and responsibilities as aunties to young women and men.

What we found convinced us that not only is the auntie relationship worth talking about, but worth examining and celebrating. Our aunties help shape our characters, our goals, our attitudes. An aunt's influence may be subtle because she may not have lived in our households. She may not even be related to us in any familial way. Aunties include our mother's and father's sisters but also those women who are part of our chosen family—trusted neighbors or close friends of one or both our parents. Just as an auntie may be blood-related or chosen, so may an auntie live long-distance or next door, be our best friend in fun or an advocate for us with our parents. Aunties may be in our lives the moment we are born or we may adopt an auntie (or she may adopt us) later on in life. It is never to late to form an auntie relationship, and, as we were told repeatedly, everyone benefits from the connection.

We lucky individuals who count aunties among our biological or chosen family members know we have benefited. Another person has loved us, given us attention, played with us perhaps when our parents didn't have time. Aunties can be lifesavers. As Ági, a seventy-five-year-old woman, told us, "It is so important to have an extended family, an aunt especially. People who don't have that are really at a disadvantage. You can cry on an aunt's shoulder or ask for advice (even if you don't take it) and get some support." Frequently aunties are the ones who step in whenever they are needed, from dropping everything when we're in a crisis to taking over our upbringing if our parents can no longer care for us.

However we know our aunties, they help form us. Aunties may have been the first adults who treated us as individuals, separate from our parents. Perhaps they provided another lifestyle to emulate, different opinions to consider, a dispassionate ear when we needed to discuss our thorniest problems and most personal (and embarrassing) concerns, or simply and most importantly, they might have been our first adult friends. Connie, a journalist, told us, "When I look back at my life to see who influenced me, I see women. They carry the family. They really do." When we stop to think about it, it is clear how the sometimes subtle, sometimes obvious roles our aunties played (or still play) deeply affect our lives.

Aunts help us know who we are. They give us a sense of identity and strength that we will take with us wherever we go. As Tessa, a marketing coordinator living in Vancouver, British Columbia, put it: "Aunts become part of the mythology. As an aunt, you don't always realize how much a part of your family you are or how important you are. But when your nieces tell stories about all the trips you've taken together and all the things they think about when times get really tough and they are looking for inner resources, somewhere along the line all those little stories and all those little things come together and provide them with that healthy sort of instinct that they need. They know they have been in a safe place once and that they can go there again."

Many cannot imagine life without these unsung heroes and mentors. As Lauren, a young woman about to get married, said of her own relationship to Karen, her mother's best friend: "I worry about something happening to my mom, but she says there will always be Karen and other people to help me and be there for me. Whenever I feel really insecure about something she tells me that. My mom and Karen have been there all my life. I don't even count the years of my life before Karen, really."

It Is Not Just a Matter of Cookies

Human relationships, especially those involving women, are frequently misrepresented in our culture. When we recall how aunties have been portrayed in popular media, we think of such characters as Auntie Mame, developed by Patrick Dennis in his book of the same name, who was eccentric and outlandish, and whose care of a child was considered inappropriate by those around her. Aunt Bea, of *The Andy Griffith Show*, was a sweet lady with a bun on her head, who was easily befuddled and could rarely make up her mind about anything. In the movie *Bell, Book and Candle*, Kim Novak's character was constantly fixing the disastrous results of her auntie's witchcraft mishaps. Auntie Em, from *The Wizard of Oz,* was rather a mystery character, present but without shape. But the common thread among these characters, consistent with what we heard from the women we interviewed, was that they all were willing to step in to care for a child when they were needed, and they all became part of that child's family.

The importance of our relationships with aunties, and their influence on our lives, does not stem from an auntie's steady supply of a child's favorite cookies, although the underlying motivation of paying attention to what a child loves is a crucial part of their care. Similarly, not all aunties are wacky eccentrics, although children can learn a lot from exposure to people with different ideas from their parents'. Rather, the auntie is much more crucial. What we heard when we examined the auntie relationship were stories about women who took their role seriously, making a conscious commitment to a child's welfare. They were willing to offer their time to play and talk, giving some backup to a tired parent or parents. Further, they were eager to offer the example of their own lives to children as they grew up, developed their own values, and made their own decisions. Not only do these women add dimension and vitality to children's lives, we heard some stories of aunties who were courageous enough to take over the act of mothering a child who needed it.

We are here to examine these sacred relationships and give them the honor they are due. Children have always needed aunties—they are part of each individual's "village." What we noted with interest when we were conducting interviews is that those who had aunties and felt influenced by them always spoke of that influence as positive. None of the women we interviewed seemed to remember any negative effect!

It Is Never Too Late

We hope the stories gathered here will encourage us all to broaden our "families"—committing to the people around us, and letting people who care about us into our lives. Dr. Bassoff quotes another writer when encouraging us to find "our people": "'Call it a clan, call it a network, call it a tribe, call it a family,' writer Jane Howard remarks. 'Whatever you call it, whoever you are, you need one.'"[9]

We may only now realize the importance of the extended family in our lives. Fortunately, it is never too late to develop one. If you are a parent, and your child doesn't have an aunt, go out together and find one. Not only can an auntie present a different perspective on life and opinions about every subject in the world, they can provide that essential link when parent and child are not communicating. Similarly, if you are an adult and you have never had an auntie, there are lots of wonderful women you can adopt. You may be surprised—there may be someone who would love a chance to get to know you better, a neighbor, a friend of your parents who has always kept an eye on you, an in-law. And if we see a child in our life—that of a close friend, for example—who can use a little more attention (and what child doesn't?) or a parent who needs some help (and what parent doesn't need a break once in a while?)— jump in and make the connection with that small person. We know of no parents who do not want more love for their child. And as we celebrate what aunties do for others, we will also discover the meaning of those relationships to the aunties themselves. Parents and children need aunties, and truthfully, aunties need them too.

Becoming an Auntie

I love being an auntie.
It's one of the best things in the world.

—DEBORAH

If a child is to keep alive his or her inborn sense of wonder, he or she needs the companionship of at least one adult who can share it, rediscovering with him or her the joy . . . of the world we live in.

—RACHEL CARSON, *The Sense of Wonder*

"You're an aunt!" may be the words we hear when a sibling or friend announces the birth of a child. Many women we interviewed who are familial aunties, sisters of the new mother or father, spoke of their surprise at their intensified sense of family, the heightened awareness of "blood ties" to a newborn niece or nephew. Similarly, a "chosen" auntie, a friend of the family asked to assist in the upbringing of the child by the parent, may feel a sense of commitment welling up within her as she realizes the valuable role she will play as an adopted member of the child's family. Whatever the relationship, either blood or honorary, many aunties recalled for us the moment of meeting that new important person in their lives and the accompanying delight and sense of responsibility in their acquired role.

When We First Met

You can remember the second and the third and the
fourth time, but there's no time like the first.
It's always there.

—SHELAGH DELANEY, *The Quotable Woman*

For many of us aunties, the first meeting with a child who is to be a special person in our lives may forever shift our self-image or our expectations of ourselves. Several women, especially those who are the youngest or only child in their immediate families or who had not had much exposure to small children, said they realized something new about themselves when first coming face-to-face with a niece or nephew. Pamela, a thirty-five-year-old landscape architect, said she was a sophomore in college when her nephew Jay was born. As the youngest in her family, she always felt uncomfortable with children, mainly because she thought she wasn't good with them. She felt that children, especially babies, always cried when they were with her.

But when her nephew was placed in her arms, she found that her self-image changed forever: "I was a little nervous when my sister-in-law asked me if

I wanted to hold him. My experience was that my nervousness always made children nervous. I didn't want to have Jay getting upset and his mother then not wanting him to be with me. But I will never forget it. It was a Saturday afternoon in the fall, and we were sitting on the couch in my brother's and sister-in-law's sunny house, and she put him into my arms. He was so trusting and relaxed. To my amazement, he seemed perfectly calm and fell asleep on my lap. We sat there for hours, my sister-in-law, Jay, and me— he just a few days old and instinctively at ease, as was his mother, and me delighted at the realization that I could bond with a child after all. It was a lovely experience, and it fundamentally changed my perception of myself. It was a real gift."

Another woman, also the youngest in her family, realized that she was not ready to take on the responsibilities of parenthood upon meeting her niece for the first time: "My brother is six years older than I am, so as children we were so far apart that our lives didn't intersect very often. When I was entering junior high school, he was entering college and leaving town. He married when I was in college and had his first child shortly after I graduated. I was very young, very immature for my age, and desperately trying to find my own identity.

"I'll never forget coming home for Christmas the year my niece was born. I had not met her yet, and since I am the youngest, I had no experience with babies. I walked into the house, which was festively decorated for the holidays, and there, lying on the floor all pink and clean and smelling like a baby was my brand new five-month-old niece. She was on a fleecy blanket in front of the fireplace.

"I'll always remember how I felt when I first saw her. I was thrilled. I immediately fell to my knees and she took my finger. But although I felt so thrilled, I was also aware of how young and irresponsible I was, and how much work it takes to raise a child. I think at that very moment I realized that although I loved my niece, I wasn't ready to have children of my own."

For another woman, Rose, a twenty-nine-year-old marketing director, being present with her sister, Lisa, at the birth of her niece started her thinking about having her own children. "Before my niece Ashley was born, I never really wanted kids. I never thought I would have kids or get married. When Ashley was born, everything changed for me.

"My other sister Marilou and Mario, who is Lisa's husband, were supposed to be the Lamaze coaches.

Lisa was told that she probably had an hour until she was fully dilated. So Mario took that opportunity to go pick someone up and bring them to the hospital. But, of course, ten or fifteen minutes later she was fully dilated. And there I was."

When Lisa, who was in labor, was asked who she wanted in the delivery room, she asked for her two sisters, Marilou and Rose. "Marilou and I were on either side of Lisa. I felt bad that Mario wasn't there, but it was incredible to be part of my niece's birth. I remember my sister squeezing my hand so hard I had ring imprints on the fingers on both sides of my ring finger. It was just amazing. There I was, thinking, 'I don't want to see all this blood,' but as she dilated, I watched, and it was amazing. The doctor turned to my sister and me and said, 'Do you want to cut the umbilical cord?' So I got to do that. The instant my niece was born, it took away my fear of having a child. That was incredible.

"Up until then I'd been thinking, 'I like kids, but I don't want them.' But after the birth and watching Ashley learn to walk and talk, I was more fascinated with children. My attitude changed. That was probably the biggest factor in helping me feel I was ready to have kids."

For Rose, the experience of children, not her own but those connected to her through her sisters, helped her make an important life decision. For Deborah, a forty-six-year-old program director, meeting a nephew for the first time was an almost magical moment in which she found a relationship that she had always missed before: "I have an absence of aunties, really, but I have three sisters and three nephews. I love being an auntie. It's one of the best things in the world. I really do believe the inspiration for that role, the importance of it, sprung from the fact that we grew up in a pretty isolated family. We had each other, but we didn't have much contact with the extended family, despite the fact that we have lots of relatives. The absence of an auntie is something that I still feel. So becoming an auntie, and having the opportunity to be in an active role as one, has been an absolutely marvelous opportunity."

When we asked what her relationship with her nephews has done for her, Deborah replied: "Sometimes when I think about my nephews or spend time with them, my heart feels so full of love and appreciation for our relationship with each other and for who these little people are in the world. It is almost overwhelming. I'm sure it's what parents feel when they have those kinds of moments. I'm not a mom myself, but it's just such a gift to have that kind of trusting, supportive, direct, loving relationship with a child. I have that with all three of them."

Deborah went on to describe the birth of one of her nephews: "When Evan was born, I went to the hospital. He was a few hours old. I remember the experience of holding him in my arms and feeling what a fairy godmother must feel like. It just came over me that I was there to give him three wishes and blessings. Obviously, I'm not the mom or the dad, but here was this little person entrusted to my arms. I held him in my arms and looked at him and said something like, 'Welcome to this world. I want you to know that anything you could ever possibly need, you can count on me to give that to you.' It was just this immediate sense that here was this little person, and he trusted me. Now he loves this story."

As Deborah later told her nephew about his birth, Mimi, a thirty-eight-year-old editor, is looking forward to sharing an emotional experience with her niece Aya when Aya grows older: "I met my niece, Aya, half an hour after she was born. She was in the nursery in a little crib under a light to keep her warm. I remember standing over her and thinking that she was the most beautiful, light-filled baby I had ever seen. When I went home later that day, I wrote a poem about those feelings, and then wrote it on a postcard that had an 'A' for Aya and a picture of an angel on it. I gave the postcard to my sister-in-law to put in Aya's new room. I really want Aya to read it when she gets older. I want her to know how she affected me, to have a sense of the import of her birth."

When we become aunties, our nieces or nephews may awaken a piece of ourselves we may not have realized was there or a love or sense of awe that we didn't know we possessed. The impression may be equally strong for the child. While most individuals don't remember the first time they met their aunties, many of us can remember when an auntie first made an impression on us.

A woman attorney had this to say about a neighbor who impressed her upon first meeting, and who became her adopted auntie: "When I was about to become an adolescent, we moved to a new neighborhood. Our neighbor was the mother of several boys. I remember when I first met her, I was struck by how lovely in appearance and personality she was. She seemed so together—she had all these children and yet she was always beautiful, both in the way she looked and the way she acted. I guess I was most impressed by her graciousness, her ability to take any situation in stride, her sense of humor no matter what was going on in her life, and her way of always making everyone feel welcome.

"I felt this immediate chemistry between us. She became a very important model for me with respect to how I wanted to act as a woman. She wasn't subservient, in fact, she was always self-possessed. I don't think I could have described it at the time, but I still admire how she always makes people feel as good as possible about themselves when they are around her. I think she adopted me somewhat because she had no daughters of her own, but also because we have similar senses of humor. I still think about her when I am trying to assess how to act in a situation. She probably doesn't know what kind of an effect she had on me. We are still friends, and I love her dearly."

Similarly, Wendy, the marketing director, recalled vividly her first meeting with her Aunt Mabel: "My first encounter with her was when I was eighteen. She wanted me to meet her for lunch at a restaurant in a fancy hotel where she was staying. I remember the first time she saw me, she looked at me and she said, 'My God, what happened to you? You are so short.' She said, 'All the women in our family are tall, what happened?' And then she said, 'Your father,' as if somehow he had made me short. I was taken aback at the time, but now I think that is so funny. I love her eccentricities.

"Anyway, we sat down for lunch and she ordered the seafood salad. Then she said to the waiter, 'Does that have prawns in it?' And he said, 'Yes, ma'am, there are prawns in it.' 'Well,' she said, 'I am allergic to prawns so please take those out.' When he started to walk away she said, 'Wait a minute. Is there crab-meat in that salad?' He said, 'Yes.' She said, 'Well, my system cannot tolerate crabmeat.' So she went through about four things that would be in a sea-food salad until all that would be left was lettuce. That was my first meeting with Aunt Mabel.

"Meeting her and our subsequent relationship definitely provided a window on a different kind of existence and way of being. She was a very unusual woman. She and her husband made a lot of money, and yet they could barely read. They were not edu-cated but they were very smart. I always found them to be so exotic. She was always 'dressed' and she was very striking. They were really wild and had a different per-spective on things than I did. I left home when I was seventeen, and my big 'rebellion' was to go to college. Mabel and my uncle were in the world in a very unusual way. It was just amazing to me that they were so successful in life and so happy, and yet could have all these odd ideas. It was a broadening experience."

We all enjoy other people's eccentricities. After all, we have none of our own, right? But beyond enjoyment, these colorful aunties provide us with something else—a tolerance for differences, a realization that all kinds of people live in the world (and may be related to us) and an understanding that personal problems or quirkiness does not take away from the value of these individuals.

Our culture doesn't often acknowledge or celebrate our auntie relationships, whether those relationships be conservative, traditional, or on the unusual side. There is a Mother's Day and a Father's Day, but no "Auntie's Day"! However, these adults and children can have profound effects on one another. As aunties, we have the opportunity to change the way we think about ourselves or to make life decisions, as Rose did when she decided she was ready to have children. And as with Deborah, the gift of being a part of a new child's life can satisfy the need for a familial relationship outside the immediate family.

Similarly, those of us who remember meeting an auntie for the first time can sense a new aspect of ourselves being tapped, or find ourselves seeing the world in a different way. The first meeting between an auntie and a young man or woman is frequently the first indicator of how much this other person will affect our attitudes, our opinions, our hearts, and our lives.

Blood Ties

There is a power in blood ties that cannot be denied.

—MARY PIPHER PH.D, *The Shelter of Each Other*

Some familial aunts, those whose siblings have had children, talked about the fierce feelings that the blood ties with their nieces and nephews stirred in them, feelings of which they were previously unaware. Dayna, a thirty-seven-year-old writer, described a "body connection" with her nieces, a feeling of a physical bond: "I wouldn't say they feel like my daughters, but they certainly feel like my blood. The love I feel for them is definitely a 'blood love.' It's in my body. We speak only every few weeks. And I know that if I were to talk to my younger niece and say, 'You know, sweetheart, I love you so much,' it would embarrass her.

"All I really want them to know, even if it's not said overtly, is that I love them, that I am there for them, and that I am interested in their lives. That I am interested to see how they grow up. I hope I can be a big sister to my nieces in a way—in a way a mother can't be."

Some aunties are struck by the physical connection when they become aware of the similarities between them and a young niece or nephew. Vicky, a fifty-six-year-old magazine editor, spoke of her surprise and pleasure when she started noticing characteristics she and her niece Sally shared: "I've always been a long-distance aunt, and I remembered visiting one Christmas and seeing a picture of her taken when she was about two. I was transfixed in front of the photo, and her mother came up behind me and said softly, 'I've seen pictures of you when you were that age. She looks just like you.' I'll never forget it. I was so proud, so happy.

"When I saw my niece I realized how much she looked like our side of the family. Really, she looked like a little miniature version of my grandfather, whom my brother and I both resemble strongly. Seeing her made me realize that even if I didn't have kids of my own that the family line would continue through these children. I'm not sure why, but for some reason that was incredibly comforting, and it relieved some pressure on me.

"When Sally was a teenager, she started coming to visit me every summer. I think this happened the second year she was visiting. I had started my own magazine, and she was helping me with an article.

She was editing a piece I had given her. I looked over at her and she started laughing, because it was so poorly written. I looked at her and it was clear we were blood-relatives. I could feel it in my gut—it was a visceral reaction.

"She read me a sentence that made no sense. Then she threw her head back and laughed at its absurdity. At that moment I realized how similar our senses of humor are. I understood on a cellular level that even though she was my brother's daughter, not my daughter, we shared certain family characteristics, both physical and personality related. We had the same DNA."

Vicky is comforted to know that her family line will be continued through her niece, even if she doesn't have children of her own. When we spoke with Rosalyn, a forty-seven-year-old producer, she told us that she finds comfort in her relationship with her niece in several ways: "We look alike. When we go out to eat, people assume she is my daughter. If you look at pictures of us at age seven it would be hard to tell us apart."

When we asked Rosalyn how it feels to be so physically similar to her niece, she said, "It's been a lesson to me. For instance, she has great self-esteem.

Sometimes I actually look at her and say to myself, 'If she has that in her blood, you have it in yours too.' Sometimes when I'm in a difficult spot I ask myself how she would react to the situation. Usually she would just put her head down and charge in. I do think about the connection a lot, that we come from the same stock. It's what I have learned from her. I truly wonder if she has learned half as much from me."

Rosalyn, by watching her niece and by recognizing their obvious similarities, is reminded of her own potential, that she may share other characteristics with her niece that she doesn't always acknowledge in herself. The amazement at and comfort in seeing parts of ourselves emerging in another human being, whether in physical characteristics or in the way we laugh, act, or view life, result in strong blood ties between aunties and their nieces and nephews. For others, the joy of these relationships springs from a feeling of belonging and a sense of being an integral part of an ongoing story.

Laura, a nurse and poet, said that what her connection with her Aunt Aggie provided, and what she is now trying to provide for her nephew, Tyler, "is a kind of tapestry of the past, the present, and an implication of the future. We were born into that fabric of love and connection, which makes us part of a whole. The little knots which make up our own lives, such as our relationships with our parents and siblings, are put into perspective. That is something I want to give to Tyler. I want him to know that he is part of that fabric. For me, knowing that is a security blanket, in a sense, when things are difficult.

"One of the things Aggie did that was so important, and that I try to do with Tyler, is to talk about ancestors. Aggie was one of ten children and she used to share her memories of her grandparents and aunts and uncles, clearly part of that huge web of connections that was so wonderful. I was named for Aggie's mother, Annie Laura, who died at age twenty-eight. I loved hearing about her and I loved hearing about Aggie's grandmother, Mercy Jane, this little Irish woman known for her hot temper, who gave birth to Aggie's father during the Civil War.

"Aunt Aggie shared countless stories—the stories about Uncle Elijah who fought in the Civil War; stories of Aggie's childhood (she was born in 1888) and about how men courted her when she was older; stories about her older sister, Aunt Viola, who ran off with the medicine man, Mr. Quigley; stories about how her family's house burned down twice. Now I try to do that with Tyler. Tyler's grandfather, my father, died before Tyler was born. But I want to make sure Tyler knows that he is part of that same web of connections.

"What's wonderful about knowing you're part of something larger is that you can never be alone after that. Your life is not solely about being an individual, it's also about these connections and knowing that you are just one little knot in the weaving. Your place is very important. Your little knot enables all the other threads to stay in place. But when you are gone, the fabric will still be there."

What comfort these relationships can provide! Vicky is relieved to know that her family line will continue for another generation. Rosalyn is reminded of her own potential. And both Laura and her nephew Tyler are fortunate to have a sense of history and the knowledge that no matter where they are, they have a tribe to belong to, a place—even if it is in the collected memories of their ancestors—to call home.

An Auntie Chosen

You hear a lot of dialogue on the death of the
American family. Families aren't dying. They're
merging into big conglomerates.

—ERMA BOMBECK, *San Francisco Examiner,* October 1, 1978

*W*hile many women fall into the auntie role
by means of a familial connection to a
child, many are chosen by the parents from their
close circle of friends. This practice has become more
prevalent in recent years. At one time, the notion of
an extended family meant grandparents, aunts,
uncles, cousins, and other blood relatives. But in our
mobile society, where adults often settle down far
from the communities in which they were raised, we
find more parents, single and married, bringing
other non-related persons into their family circle.

Ultimately, it does not matter to the children
involved that these people are not blood-related. As
Dr. Mary Pipher writes in her book, *The Shelter of Each
Other:* "For many people, friends become family. Family is a collection of people who pool resources and
help each other over the long haul. Families love
one another even when that requires sacrifice. Family

means that if you disagree, you still stay together."[10] Women chosen for this auntie role have the potential to form especially strong relationships with their adopted nieces and nephews as they are handpicked by the parents to help care for their child. Similarly, as Dr. Pipher suggests, these aunties who are close friends of the parents may actually feel more like family, with similar viewpoints and values of the parents. These women may be selected in a formal capacity as a godmother or they may be more informally brought into a child's care and upbringing. Additionally, as children grow up and grow older, they might also find aunties of their own choosing.

Linda, a corporate executive on the West Coast, is an auntie to several of her friends' children. "I have six children who call me 'auntie,' none of whom are blood related. I have three girls, ages ten, nine, and four, and three boys, ages seven, five, and two. So far the children's gender has not really affected how I treat them, but I really try to be aware of who each individual child is and to treat them differently from one another. I have a really different relationship with each kid."

Once that relationship is established, it can grow separately from the original relationship the auntie had to the parents of the child. Witness Linda's relationship with her adopted niece, Zoe: "Zoe is the daughter of my ex-husband's brother. I am her godmother. I thought that was a really nice way for them to honor me and make me more a part of their family, since he is her blood uncle and already has a role in her life.

"But that makes it interesting, because I am a part of their family, but divorced from Zoe's 'real' uncle. That presents some long-term issues. Zoe was concerned that my divorce would mean a loss to her somehow because our original connection through her uncle had been removed. She would ask me questions like, 'Does this mean that you won't come to my wedding?' She was fast-forwarding to these crucial events. I told her, 'I will be wherever I am supposed to be, whenever I am supposed to be there, don't you worry. We will both be there and it will be just great.'"

While some aunties are chosen as godmothers or special aunties and start their relationship with great intention and commitment, some aunties fall into the role unexpectedly. Erica and Vanessa, now twenty-one and eighteen, respectively, told us dozens of stories about their adopted aunties, Sandy and

Kaki (so named by Vanessa who, as a baby, couldn't say "Katherine"). Vanessa began: "Our parents got divorced when we were very, very small. I was four months old, and Erica was four years old. Our mother had little money and two very small children. These two women, Sandy and Kaki, who went to our church, were living in a house together. They had an extra room to rent, and the three of us moved into it."

What started out as a business arrangement quickly became something much richer to these two little girls. Vanessa said, "They probably didn't plan on loving us as much as they did. Sandy and I have talked about what a leap of faith it was for the two of them to allow these two very, very small children—"

"—into their completely adult and docile life." Erica interrupted, laughing. "We had to get up early for school, while they were still asleep. Mom was always saying to us, 'Quiet in the morning, quiet in the morning,' but I can't imagine that we did very well."

Erica and Vanessa went on to tell us how Sandy and Kaki, neither of whom had children, became a vital part of their lives, sharing everything from working together in their enormous kitchen to learning Shakespeare quotes to playing dominoes. Sometimes the two women got up in the middle of the night with the children so the girls' mother could sleep. Erica laughed as she recalled one of Kaki's favorite stories about that time: "Once Kaki was baby-sitting the two of us, and she and I were playing dominoes. I was five at the time. Vanessa had a dirty diaper, and Kaki had never changed a diaper in her life. I took her step-by-step through changing the diaper. Kaki has kids now, and she talks about how she knows how to change diapers all because of Vanessa and me."

Erica and Vanessa lived with Kaki and Sandy for six years, until their mother remarried. But they each recognize the enormous influence that those two aunties had on them individually and on their relationship together. Erica credits her aunties with her love of cooking for friends: "We spent a lot of time in the kitchen. We baked everything. We always had dinner together. I think that's why I'm always having my friends over to my house and cooking for them."

Vanessa commented that her aunties helped the relationship between her and Erica by providing a sympathetic ear and empathetic stories: "There was strain and tension in our relationship as children. We didn't fight, but basically what would happen is that Erica would be mean to me, as siblings some-times can be, and I would become sad about it, because I really looked up to her as my older sister.

"Sandy has a sister, and they are about the same distance apart in age as Erica and I. She wouldn't exactly give me advice, but she would say really comforting things to me. One time—I don't remember why Erica wasn't there—I was in Sandy's room. I was talking to her about how sad I was, and she told me about how she and her sister had not gotten along and that now they were very close. She said to me, 'I know that this may not make sense to you now, but you and your sister will be friends. The older you get the easier it is to appreciate each other. I can tell that you will be able to be friends. You are just going to have to be patient until Erica is able to care about you the way that you want her to.'

"At the time I thought, 'No, Erica just doesn't like me.' But Sandy's words stuck with me, and I still remember thinking, 'Maybe she is right. That would be great if Erica and I turned out like Sandy and her sister.' Sandy had a lot of influence and she was sort of an advocate. Not necessarily against Erica, whom she loved dearly. But she helped me out a lot, in feeling that there was hope for our friendship." At which point, Erica and Vanessa smiled at each other and said simultaneously "And she was right."

Of course, it is not only children who need the love of an older person, someone to talk to and depend on for empathy and advice. It is never too late to adopt (or be adopted by) an auntie. Betsy, a fifty-five-year-old teacher, didn't have a strong aunt in her childhood. "Our family is quite small. Both my parents had only one sibling, and my father's brother died during the Second World War. I wasn't particularly close to my mother's brother's wife. So I grew up with my mother and her best friend (whom I still remember as an extraordinary woman) as my primary female role models. Today I live halfway across the continent from my hometown.

"My best friend has an aunt who is about the same age as my mom. She is a super auntie to her many siblings' children. Over the years I've gotten to know her quite well and have grown very fond of her. She's even met my mother. I am an honorary auntie to my best friend's two-year-old daughter, and as I watch our relationship grow and realize how important it is to me, and hopefully will be to my honorary niece, I have also watched how important this woman is to me. She is beautiful—stunning, really, a real show-stopper. She is gracious and charming and despite her diminutive stature when she walks into a room, everyone notices. She has shown me that I don't have to worry about growing old, that elderly women can be beautiful. I've spent many hours with her talking about what her life was like growing up as a Jew in Europe during World War II and then traveling around the world. We talk about everything: men, love, life, commitment, all the things I face as an adult woman. She is always there with a kind word and an intelligent perspective. The other day I realized how important she is to me and how much she has enriched my life. I asked her if she would be my honorary aunt. When she said yes, I was thrilled. I hope she knows what it means to me."

More love is always better, and taking the task of "aunting" to heart is a pronounced act of love for a child—or an adult, for that matter. Children who know that someone loves them and thinks about them when she isn't "required" to do so, as parents are, will learn that they are worthy of love. Similarly, adult nieces and nephews who feel that another person cares for them, takes time out for them even when not required to do so, makes a commitment to be a friend, a caretaker, or even a good listener to them, are enriched by the experience and are better equipped to deal with life ahead.

A Special Task, A Special Reward

Women are the real architects of society.

—HARRIET BEECHER STOWE, *Atlantic Monthly,* 1864

*W*hether born to the job or chosen as honorary aunties, many aunties feel particular responsibilities toward their relationship with that child or young adult, responsibilities separate from their relationship with the boy's or girl's parents. As we were interviewing aunties, we asked them what they thought their role entailed. What does it really mean to be an auntie?

Linda, the corporate executive with six adopted nieces and nephews, had been asked to be a godmother for three children and an honorary aunt to three more. She takes her role as a godmother and auntie quite seriously and has considered the differences and similarities between those roles: "I think 'honorary aunt' is one thing, that because of your relationship with the family in general it's a loving and respectful title that makes you part of the family and also indicates to the children that you are someone special to the family. You are the mother's best friend. You are going to be at all the holiday dinners, for example. But 'godmother,' I think, is a very special designation that the parents have thought about in response to the question of who they want to have a relationship with their child. Not incidentally, but specifically. When they ask me, 'Would you do this?' I ask, 'What does this mean to you as parents?'

"All of them have answered in one way or another that they intended that I have a special relationship with the child. Now that I am an experienced godmother, I say to any new 'candidates,' 'This means that I will have an independent relationship with the child and that I will be able to say whatever I need to say to the child. You need to let us have our own relationship. She (or he) and I will work out any problems. We need to have our disagreements in our relationship, and you don't need to tell me how to behave around the child and you don't need to tell the child how to behave around me.'"

Although the degree of formality connoted by the titles "auntie" and "godmother" may differ, Linda nevertheless feels that the role of both is the same: "I have given this a lot of thought and I feel like my job as either the godmother or the auntie would be the same. My role is to be an adult friend and not to be a parent. A parent is someone who is much more of an active counselor, a guide, someone who is disciplining and teaching in a very proactive way. Not that I wouldn't participate in any of those activities, but I feel like my job is to not be judgmental, not to take every opportunity to teach them something, but to be a real friend and to wait and find out what they have to say. Sometimes the parents are so aware of every opportunity to teach or discipline, whether their child is learning to count, learning the ABC's, or learning not to put their elbows on the table. Sometimes I have a hard time restraining myself, because I can be sort of an authoritarian person, but I don't want the children to see me as just another grownup who is trying to tell them how it is.

"I think what the kid gets out of it is that I'm not a teacher, a parent, or the mother of a friend, but I am going to treat them like an equal and demand that they have a real relationship with me. When I say 'real relationship,' I mean that they have to be nice to me and treat me fairly. They have to learn that I'm not going to take abuse from them, that just because I am a grownup doesn't mean they can treat me badly. They also have to make an effort and earn my respect. Of course, I make allowances for them because they are children. I don't expect them to be emotionally mature, and it is okay with me if they act out. I'm sorry if it makes them feel bad but I do tell them whenever they hurt my feelings. Often I say it in a joking way, but I don't put up with lots of bad behavior."

Linda contributes to her "children's" upbringing by being a friend and showing them the meaning of friendship and the right way to treat others. Many women give their role serious thought in order to contribute as much as possible to the quality of a niece's or nephew's life. Robin, a psychologist and minister, was a single woman with no children of her own when her younger sister shared the news that she and her husband were expecting their first child. "I felt this wonderful sense of joy and anticipation that I was being given the gift of investing in a little one's life who was going to be genetically connected to me. I wasn't sure whether I'd eventually marry or have children so my sister's pregnancy represented a unique new role for me as 'Aunt Robin.'

"I think as I anticipated the birth of that child, I began to formulate the special role I hoped I would have in his or her life. I knew I wanted to be very *intentional* about the time invested in the life of my niece or nephew and the quality of those moments together.

"That particular sister ended up having two daughters and one son. From the time my nieces and nephews were tiny, they were in my arms on frequent occasions, even though I had a highly demanding ministry and a lot of travel at that time in my profession.

"We began a tradition when each child was about two years old which was called 'Aunt Robin dates.' These 'dates' would usually be about once a month and they looked like this: They lasted twenty-four hours because I wanted to insure that it would be an over-nighter—open-ended enough that we could just spend those extra hours at night or in the morning talking about anything they wanted to explore, giggle about, cry about, or learn. During our 'dates' the rule was that they could wear anything they wanted to wear, they got to pick what we would do on our date, and they could eat any kind of food they wanted for a meal, including popcorn or pizza for breakfast!

"How long did our little tradition last? Well, I think the dates went right into their early adolescence. It was an amazing investment of time, money, and sometimes sheer energy to drive the one-hundred twenty-five miles each way to make those dates a reality—but I wouldn't change a moment of those memories. And neither would they. Somewhere at about sixteen they began to take Aunt Robin on dates and pay for the pizza and movies as a treat to me!"

While Robin has provided a safe place for her nieces and nephews to talk and explore their interests, Tessa, the marketing coordinator, sees herself as a "back-up" caregiver. She equates her responsibility as an aunt with being ever ready to take in a child who needs help, and wants her nieces and nephews to feel that they always have a safe place to go as long as she is around: "I really have enjoyed being an aunt. I see myself as custodian of them; that is, if anything should happen to their parents, I wouldn't even think twice, if they were young, I would take them in. As they become older, I want them to know they are always welcome at my home, with their children, with their problems, and all of that sort of thing. That's one of the things that my mother instilled in us when we were growing up, that we would look out for each other. As a family we are very close, although we are scattered over many countries."

All these women are making themselves available to, and committing to enriching the lives of, the children they "aunt." Offering ourselves to this commitment, opening up to this relationship in which we may be called upon to make the effort, carries an important reward—a sense of belonging and a satisfaction in knowing our importance in a child's life. Theresa, a thirty-eight-year-old stockbroker, saw her niece as bringing her closer to her brother and sister-in-law: "When she was born, I realized in an instant that this child would bring me closer to my brother (whom I adored but never saw) and his new wife, whom I hardly knew and who was a little intimidating. But over the years the kids brought the entire family closer together. The birthday parties, the holiday meals, the phone calls—just sharing in the children's growing up—were all catalysts in bringing us together. Without the kids we probably would have lived very separate lives."

Similarly, Rosalyn, whose niece was one of the reasons she moved from Kansas City to Los Angeles, talked about how her niece Rosa's birth brought her family closer just when she expected it to become more distant: "My niece was conceived within weeks of my mother's death. If you had asked me at that time, I would have said that after my mother died, we would all become less close. But it has not been that way at all. If anything, we are all closer now. Rosa, who is named after my mother, is a big part of that. The connection is always there, even though Mother never met her. That has left all of us with a greater responsibility to passing on the memories."

Linda, who is so devoted to her adopted nieces and nephews, finds great reward for her devotion to them. She has the satisfaction of "paying back" the love and attention lavished on her as a child by her own Aunt Marguerite, who to this day remains an important person in her life. Linda additionally is benefitted by being a member of many families: "What are the benefits I receive? I feel like you can never have too many people to love or to be loved by, and I am part of all these families because I am either the godmother or the auntie. So on all the big occasions I get to sit in the front row because I am someone special. And that makes me feel really good and important. I have artwork for my refrigerator. I get school pictures, I get valentines. My cat gets birthday cards. I feel really loved. And that's a nice thing."

She continues, with a grin, "Of course, the adults who are grateful for the things I have done for their children are always busy trying to be nice to me! I have explained to them that they don't need to do these things for me as a payback for the things I have done for their children, but I still get much better gifts now than before I was a godmother!"

More importantly, Linda has found that adoption into these families has brought her more intangible gifts: "Last year, when I was having a difficult divorce, the mothers of my three official godchildren took me to lunch. That was really a fun thing. Just us grownups. It was really nice of them. Similarly, as a result of my being Katie's godmother, Lori, Katie's mother, invited me to be in the room when she gave birth to her next baby. So that was really great because I am not going to have any children of my own. When Austin was born I was the third person to hold him. We have a very special relationship because of that. I have learned that it is amazing how much you can love someone. As I am being their adult friend when they are children I see that, when I am old, they will be my adult friends. Just like my Aunt Marguerite used to always think of me, I now think of her. I now send roses to her on Valentine's Day. I try to be there for her, because she was there for me."

Like her Aunt Marguerite, Linda will have friends for life in these children. Similarly, Robin experienced great joy and delight as her two oldest nieces were recently married in large church weddings. "I gave the opening prayer at the ceremony of my oldest niece, which included my gratitude for my niece Jolene's presence in my life: 'Father, I thank you for the astounding gift you graced my own life with the day that Jolene was born. I thank you for the joy, the wonder, the sensitivity, and the complete delight that began the day she made me her Aunt Robin by her entrance into the world.'"

Robin remembers a particularly poignant conversation she had with her niece's father on the afternoon of the wedding celebration. "My sister and brother-in-law had gone through a very painful and complicated divorce when my nieces were four and six and my nephew was about a year old. A lot of bitterness, anger, and disappointment clouded most of our family gatherings as we all struggled to somehow do damage control with the children. That afternoon my former brother-in-law took me aside and thanked me for the significant, supportive role I had held in the lives of the children through all those years of growing up. There was a warm hug of grateful recognition that to this day brings tears to my eyes as I remember it."

A good auntie knows the value she can add to a

child's life and proceeds with thoughtfulness and a sense of responsibility. Knowing that you have contributed to the future and that you are helping form a decent, responsible, and confident child is reward enough. However, as is so often the case when we give of ourselves, we also receive as much or more than we give, as we find ourselves becoming part of other families or even closer to our own.

Long Distance Aunties

I love sending packages to her, and she loves receiving them. If she lived next door, we wouldn't do that.

—SHERRY POWELL, contributor

Many of us are physically distant from our nieces and nephews. However, that has not stopped aunties from maintaining close, rewarding relationships with the children who are important to them. We talked to many women who found ways to keep the relationship lively and nurturing. Donna, a forty-eight-year-old journalist who lives on the West Coast, made a conscious decision to become close to her niece and nephew, who live on Long Island. As she told us, "My niece was about eight weeks old when I first met her, and I was there for my nephew's birth. I tried to schedule my vacation around his due date. The day I was scheduled to leave, my sister-in-law gave birth, so I was able to be one of the first people to hold him.

"I made it a point to try to be there for their birthdays. For my niece, I was there for every birthday for the first five years of her life. Then for the first couple of years when my nephew was an infant

I didn't do that but when he was about four or five, I started doing that with him too."

When Donna visits on these occasions, she exerts the effort to create memorable occasions for the children, events that reflect their interests and development: "I think it was on my niece's fifth birthday, we had a makeup party. We had it in the backyard, and everybody had a 'station'—her mom did nails, another aunt did something else. I was there for that party and she and I were one station—I think we did hair. She really remembers that I was there for her makeup party. I think it was special to her."

Donna has managed to create a tradition with her niece and nephew even though she is so far away: "I stay with my mom because she has a condominium and I have my own bedroom, but they always want to spend one night with me alone. That time together is really important to them.

"The last time my niece I did that, she was experiencing pre-adolescence. We talked pretty intimately about bodies and changes. I felt really very close to her right then. It's great. I really like this little time, this time we have late at night where we kind of cuddle up and talk. We read teen magazines, she brings all her teen magazines into bed and we look

63

at them and we talk about boys and such things.

"Because there's two of them, I always try to give them each their day on my visits—time with me alone where nobody bothers us, and where my attention is not divided. My nephew is a computer nut, so I brought my laptop back with me last time I visited. That was where we connected. He loved the laptop and he taught me things on it. We played on it together. That was our time with each other.

"We also talk on the phone a lot. My brother and sister-in-law and I are quite close, and we talk at least once a week, maybe more, on the phone. I always make sure I say hello to my niece and nephew when I'm on the phone with their parents. Now they know my voice, so I don't have to identify myself, I've never had to identify myself. I just say hi and they know who I am. I deliberately made the connection with them early in their lives."

We can hold an important position in our nieces' and nephews' lives, even from many time zones away. Where we are physically does not matter, so long as we are dedicated to honoring the auntie relationship. Linda has the commitment to make it work with Zoe, one of her honorary nieces, who lives in England: "Although it is a challenge to keep in touch with her, we have an imaginative correspondence with each other through our cats, which has worked really well. For instance, Zoe will let me know things by pretending her cat is writing a letter to my cat. I think Zoe can tell me lots of things through her cat, Nutmeg, that she would feel uncomfortable telling me in other ways. Similarly, my cat, Marty, can give Zoe lots of advice through Nutmeg.

"Zoe is ten. She is a very imaginative little girl and very artistic. Her letters from Nutmeg are all illustrated. They are just beautiful, with all these little drawings and poems about Nutmeg and the adventures he has had. Of course, Nutmeg is a 'supercat' that has many powers and can do many things that an ordinary cat couldn't do, including express his feelings. Over a couple of years this has developed into an interesting correspondence in which Nutmeg tells my cat, Marty, the ways in which he is concerned about Zoe."

Because they are accustomed to communicating in writing, Linda and Zoe have had to recover from the awkwardness of actually seeing each other: "When she and I speak on the phone, or when we're face-to-face, I think that there is a shyness because of the physical distance between us. We haven't laid eyes on each other in a year. When I visited her, she was so excited to see me that she was completely tongue-tied for the first couple of hours. Later she said, 'I have all these things to tell you, but when I saw you I couldn't remember one thing to say.' The distance presents a challenge in my relationship with her."

Although physical presence helps cement any relationship, aunties have found ways to adapt to separation. One auntie we interviewed is tied to her nieces and nephews via the Internet. By phone, fax and yes, even mail (people still write letters!), aunties keep in touch with their children, and keep their connection alive with visits for special occasions. Although it may take a while to adapt to physical closeness after that separation, a little patience and understanding on the auntie's part will overcome a child's shyness and unleash the excitement he or she has contained over an auntie's visit. As these women have indicated, an auntie can be an intimate member of a child's family, no matter where she lives. With some effort and focus, we can enjoy the auntie connection regardless of our location.

Getting to Know You

Challenges make you discover things about yourself
that you never really knew. They're what make
the instrument stretch—
what make you go beyond the norm.
—CICELY TYSON, *The Quotable Woman*

$\mathcal{S}$ome aunties get involved with their charges early on, when the child is still a baby. And although they are excited by the opportunity to get to know a child one-on-one, many women we talked with reported feeling a bit (or very) scared about the responsibility of being alone with a young girl or boy. Rose, after becoming an aunt for the first time, talked about her first "date" with her baby niece Ashley: "I remember the first time I was left alone with Ashley. I just about died. I was the only one in the apartment. My sister was probably only gone for all of half an hour, but the baby screamed from the moment Lisa left until the moment she came back."

This sense of anxiety is not limited to when the children are babies. As Deborah, forty-six and an aunt to three nephews, told us: "I actually ended up taking these boys to New York this summer on my own. My sister was planning on going with me, and then she got sick, so it was a few days later before she joined me. It was a monumentary scare for me."

Challenging situations can be very rewarding when we learn we are capable of surviving them. Deborah said that although her trip with three boys was rather daunting, she also realized "that their parents trusted me with these children's lives. And the kids trusted me. It was absolute. I think that's a really strong sign of the kind of depth that we have experienced with each other." Deborah has the pleasure of knowing that she has established a connection with the children, which she had been hoping and working for as they grew up.

Many aunties we spoke with said a one-on-one relationship with their nieces or nephews kept improving if they were able to spend some time alone together, apart from other adults and children. Theresa, the stockbroker, talked about how her relationship with both of her nieces developed separately over the years: "When the girls were young, I didn't feel that we had a full relationship. It wasn't until the children started to get older and were capable of a more complex connection that the relationship blossomed. It was built slowly. I really didn't know my nieces until they were adolescents. When they were very young, our relationship was kind of superficial, mainly because I didn't know how to be an aunt. I was so busy trying to establish my career that I didn't have time for them. When they got older I felt like I wanted them to come out (we live on opposite coasts) and spend some time with me. I wanted to get to know them. One at a time they started coming out and spending two to three weeks with me each summer."

Dayna, now a thirty-seven-year-old writer, had a similar fear of not being a "good enough" auntie, which at first stood in the way of her reaching out to her older niece: "I was so busy finding myself, as one is at twenty years old. I don't think I knew how to be an aunt to her. I remember one time we got into some sort of fight. I remember I actually said these words, which shocked me: 'Stop acting like such a child. We will not discuss it any further until you can act more like a grownup.' After I said that I remember thinking, 'She isn't a grownup.' Then I realized that neither was I. I didn't consider myself an adult then. Not until I was in my thirties did I start to really feel like I was growing up. I think I was worried that because I was young and troubled, going through a lot of hard times, that I might have set the stage for a negative relationship with her. That worried me and I think to compensate I stayed away a little bit.

"It wasn't until the last few years that I felt like maybe I knew a bit more of how to be a good aunt. She is now at that very tough age. She is discovering boys. She has lots of secrets. She might open up to me more if I was there more. I almost had them visit this summer, but my sister couldn't make it work. But I was thrilled by the idea and I am going to try to get them to come out next summer and spend at least a week with me."

As Theresa and Dayna recalled, many times aunties have to overcome their own "growing up" issues or the fear that they won't be good aunts, before they can take on the role of being an auntie. However, whether they felt like competent aunts or not, their initial contact was important in establishing a closer relationship later on. Likewise, individual attention is very important in establishing a close tie with a child. Theresa has gotten to know her nieces as they visit her separately every summer. She realizes that her nieces like it that way too. "I asked them if they wanted to visit together next year, but they said they wanted to come out separately. It's kind of stressful for me because then I have house guests for several months, but it's worth it. We have a ball. They are very different. They need different things from me."

Whatever the discomfort, the effort pays off in the end, according to the aunties we interviewed. Robin is now the aunt of four nieces and two nephews. She is currently going through the end of an era in their lives. "The two oldest nieces recently got married and I am learning how to have 'nephews-in-law'—we are sharing our times together now with extended family. As my nieces have children of their own, I anticipate I will hold a special place in the lives of my great-nieces and nephews. But I have to admit that while I know that this will be a special time too, I recognize that our unique one-on-one relationship is coming to an end. It's hard to let go of that. I think I am experiencing 'empty nest'!"

Surrogate Children

Since I wasn't ready for a child myself,
I was able to experience some of the pleasures
by taking on the role of "aunt."
—JOAN K. PETERS, *When Mothers Work*

*W*hile many women of all ages and circumstances talked to us about the importance of the auntie relationship, women who were childless frequently looked to their connection to a niece or nephew, whether familial or honorary, to fulfill a need of their own. Dr. Evelyn Bassoff, in her book *Cherishing Our Daughters*, notes "[t]he renowned psychologist Erik Erikson explained that the developmental task for all healthy adults is to become 'generative'—to contribute in significant ways to the well-being of the next generation—lest they feel stagnant and incomplete."[11] Making a connection with a child in our lives can bring us the joy and satisfaction of knowing that we have made a difference to the next generation, especially if we have no children of our own or our children are grown.

Many women today choose not to have children or are unable to do so. For those who choose not to, their decision may not be celebrated by the rest of their families. One woman who decided not to have children laughingly recalled how grateful she felt when she became an auntie, because it took the pressure off her to provide grandchildren! Then, as she grew older, she was able to take pleasure in watching the children's development.

This arrangement works well for children and their parents too. Commentators are noting the increasing need for "family." As Dr. Bassoff writes: "Within the last few years, sociologists are reporting, American families have begun to place greater emphasis on family traditions and to go out of their way to be together for holidays. This renewed longing to be with our families suggests that we are ready to depend on each other again. . . . What we and our children need are people who are there for us, not just this week but also next week, next month, next year and in the years to come." Dr. Bassoff goes on to say that this type of "consistent caring" can be partially provided by the many adults who are choosing not to have children, thereby freeing "them up to nurture the children of their siblings or close friends."[12]

Connie, a journalist, chose not to have children. She told us that she appreciates the role her nieces and nephews play in her life, not only because she loves being a part of their lives but also because they help mark stages in her own life: "It was wonderful for me to have these nieces and nephews. Not only did I get to 'do the holidays' with them, but it has given me a sense of my own maturing and aging, which parents have, but nonparents don't. I went to all the college graduations and all the weddings. These are rites of passage that parents are so aware of, while I tend to think of myself as forever twenty-seven. That's okay, but you do have to realize the importance of generations and why a grandchild is very different from a child. It's the first time you are seeing your lineage continued. It's helped me be the age I am and where I am."

While Connie finds that the maturation of the children in her life helps her to mark milestones in her own life, Rosalyn, forty-seven, has found that her being single contributes to her ability to have a more undefined friendship role with her niece: "One of the interesting things about our relationship is that there is a certain amount of agelessness to it. It has to do with my being unmarried. I can remember a conversation we had just when she was beginning to put things together. I remember it so vividly, sitting in a McDonald's. She was asking if my father was married, if my brother was married, and so on. She perceived me as younger than her father because I am not married. I saw her looking at me and saying, 'You're not a grownup.' We have laughed a lot about that. It's been part of the basis of our friendship. I have to call it a friendship, in that I don't treat her like a child and she doesn't treat me like a grownup. It's given me the chance to play again. To think things through the way a child does. And because of our honesty and the fact that I am not a parent, I think we do that extremely well.

"Not having parental responsibility does make a difference. I don't want to say I am irresponsible, because I think I play a part in her life, but I can be more of an explorer with her, maybe, in terms of the questions. I can offer a different perspective. Because I am not with her on a daily basis, we are able to look at issues, look at problems and questions, and really solve them. It's more a matter of tackling things together than saying, 'This is my viewpoint and this is your viewpoint.'"

For women who know they want children but have not yet had them, the relationship with another person's child can help fulfill that desire. Karen, an attorney who adopted her own child in recent years, talked about how her relationship with her best friend's daughter Lauren relieved the internal pressure she felt about having children: "I always wanted to be a parent and I always related well to kids. When I met Pat, who became my best friend, I was single and not quite thirty. I had a big career, in which I was very happy, but I hadn't had kids, and that felt like a huge gap in my life. When Pat and I became friends, to get to be with Lauren was such a treat for me, even in the early years when she was quite young. It was great for me to be able to share in her growing up."

These days Karen feels that Lauren, now an adult woman about to be married, is like her own daughter: "What I got early on from Lauren was a feeling of connection and being able to share in watching somebody grow up. Lauren and her mom and I made a family. There are lots of things that we share. I remember the years I was trying to get pregnant. When I adopted Sam, Lauren supported me through all of that. The years that were hard for me, I got so much love and support from her. I feel that she is Sam's sister. I learned a lot about being a parent to Sam by watching how Pat was a parent to Lauren. Their relationship is so great."

For women who never had children, taking on the role of an aunt can become a crucial part of their lives. Ági told us that being an aunt "was a very important role. I always wanted to have children. I couldn't have them, but it was a lifelong quest for me to be involved in the next generation, and the next generation. Right now I am seventy-five, so already we are a four-generation family. We used to be five, but since my mother died several years ago, my sister and I and my husband are the oldest generation. But I am connected with all the nieces and nephews and grandnieces and grandnephews and so on. I love them all differently. The more love I have, the more they come into my life. Thanks to my sister and my nieces and my nephews, I feel even more love in me."

Not only are we prominent in the lives of the children who call us auntie, but they have a momentous role in how we view our lives, and as Ági points out, how much love we carry in us. Many of the women we spoke to voiced their belief that becoming an integral part of a child's life is an honor and a privilege. Just as aunties fill in the gaps for the children whom they love, so those children fill in the gaps for those who are lucky enough to be aunties.

Goody, the owner of a hotel and coffeehouse, who enjoyed the love and attention of several aunties, described the joy of being an auntie herself: "I don't think you have to have children in today's world at all. But it is really important to have an extended family. If a woman doesn't have a niece, she should get one. Borrow one from somebody else. I think that someday you really do need them." In fact, it may be difficult to decide just who benefits the most.

Aunties' Gifts

I really believe that to a child, love is in the details.
Love is the attention to those small things,
because to a child, these small things are big things.

—LAURA

*Some people are your relatives but others are your
ancestors, and you choose the ones you want to have as
ancestors. You create yourself out of those values.*

—RALPH ELLISON, *Time*, 1964

*A*unties offer an enormous and varied set of
gifts—from acceptance and advice to a listening ear and friendship. They may offer us a
different perspective from which to consider life or
a safe harbor from our parents' disapproval. This all
adds up to a lot of acceptance, safety, and support,
and no child can have too much of those things.
Based on our interviews with aunties and nieces everywhere, we confirmed our suspicion that it does
indeed take a village to raise a child, and that aunties
are a conspicuous and substantial part of the village's
"elder" population.

Relief from Expectations

*[P]arenthood is not a second childhood, and children
are not miniature versions of ourselves. From the
beginning, they are individuals who must be respected
for who they are and are meant to become.*

—HILLARY RODHAM CLINTON, *It Takes a Village*

*A*ll children need to be loved by their parents. They also need to be subject to the rules and limitations imposed by those responsible for their safety and development. But every child also needs a break from those rules and, many times, the expectations that underlie them. As Dorothy Corkille Briggs warns parents in her book, *Your Child's Self-Esteem:* "Each of us sees our children to some degree through a haze of filters born of our past experiences, personal needs, and cultural values. They all combine to form a network of expectations. And these expectations become yardsticks by which we measure a child."[13]

While parents can examine their expectations for themselves, many aunts feel their role is to provide some relief from parental goals. Some parents are sufficiently aware of their own agendas for their children, and choose a person from among their friends to counter balance those goals. Linda feels that her friend Lisa purposely chose her to be in her son Alexander's life to balance out the expectations that Lisa and her husband had for their child.

Linda told us: "Lisa picked me specifically because she could foresee that I would be valuable to her in her parenting of Alexander. For instance, she has already said many times, 'When he asks me the hard questions about sex, I am going to send him directly to your house.' She isn't kidding. I think she is going to send him to me to introduce him to the big wide world. She sees me as his Auntie Mame—someone who is going to think it is okay if he goes to the nudist colony. I think she sees my relationship with him as another anchor in her parenting. She can turn to me for reassurance that everything is going to be all right if her son does something 'different.'

"She and her husband are more traditional. They would already have him pre-enrolled in Stanford and Harvard if they could, whereas my sense is that maybe he won't like that road. He might do something else, and it's going to be okay. I think she is relying on me very much."

Wendy, in her fifties, also feels that she can take some of the pressure off her niece: "She is a very independent, very bright child. She is the child of two very bright parents who are trying really hard to do a good job. She is sort of precocious. Sometimes I feel that what I need to do is help her be a little kid. She should not be so worried about achieving and doing and concerns like that. She feels a lot of pressure from her parents."

This is not to say that by having expectations, parents are hurting their children. Parents often feel daunted by the difficulties of raising a good person who will also be capable of self-support. Raising a functional and morally conscious child is a multidimensional and complicated task, and no parent is going to do a perfect job. Having other trusted individuals help to develop other necessary dimensions, such as the importance of enjoying what one does and learning to measure and respect one's own accomplishments separate from a parent's (or any other person's) expectations, is essential, especially in those difficult times when children are trying to figure out who they are as individuals.

Olivia, the writer, told us about how her Aunt Anne relieved some of those expectations for her in her teen years, without ever even talking about them. "I had kind of a hard time with my mother as all thirteen-year-olds probably do. We never talked about that, Anne and I, not until long after my mother died. At the time, I just knew there was support there from Anne, that I wouldn't be judged. I never went to her complaining about a conversation with my mother or anything like that. There wasn't a lot of talking in our relationship—it was mostly that I felt free with her. I knew that I was welcome. She was more demonstrative than my mother, certainly. Every time I saw her we hugged. I really don't remember that happening with my mother. Maybe I felt a little more needed by my aunt.

"She was also more detached than my mother was. I really think my mother saw me as such a reflection of herself. I was sensitive anyway, and I felt overwhelmed by having to live up to that. With Anne I just felt anything I did was fine. She was so much more easygoing. She just kind of rolled with it, whereas my mother was pretty intense. It was just so comfortable."

The feeling of being accepted as we are, free of criticism and guilt, helps us to be creative and flexible as adults. When we were talking to Deborah, the forty-six-year-old program manager, she mentioned that Barbara Sher's book *WishCraft* provides a model for the kind of supportive person she wishes to be with her nephews: "Sher said something about how great it would have been if, when we were kids, and we came home with an interest, such as filmmaking, our parents had said, 'Oh, great! Here's a camera. Here's how you do it. That's just wonderful. Let me know if you need any help.' The idea is that parents should be supportive of the child's interest, whatever it is. When two weeks later, the kid decides she wants to be an archeologist, there also wouldn't be any of those comments like, 'I thought you wanted to be a filmmaker. I just spent my money on a camera for you.' They would just be endlessly supportive of whatever interests were developing.

"I was inspired by that concept and also sad that we generally don't get to experience that. It came to mind, however, in this auntie role, and I think this is a place where it's probably easier to be tolerant of different interests than a parent might be. I feel like that's how I can nurture these kids. Whatever they are interested in, I am able to go along and help influence that—find them things, add to it, make connections, whatever little opportunities I see. If I buy a kid a baseball because I know at that moment that's what he's interested in, and next week he's interested in something completely different, that's fine with me. I feel no judgment or intolerance about who he is. I think that's part of why we have this relationship.

"Parents have expectations. I obviously have expectations too, in the sense that I want these kids to succeed and be good people and all that. Nevertheless, as far as I am concerned, they can express whatever it is and I am going to be supportive of it. To the best of my ability, I try to honor that when I give gifts too. Sometimes it's a matter of finding a baseball cap or a bookmark. Who really cares about a bookmark? But I found one with electric guitars on it, which my nephew Reuben is interested in. It was the perfect thing for him, and he was pleased and started to use it. It wasn't a big deal, but he was happy with it."

Even something as small as a bookmark with electric guitars on it can make children feel that they are being recognized as individuals, that their interests are being acknowledged. To a parent who is busy with a child's care and feeding and moral upbringing, it may be difficult to separate out and honor that child's unique identity. However, the ratification of other adults—in particular, a child's aunties—of the importance of the child's dreams and personality, is crucial to their development as happy, confident adults. Aunties often perform the role of mirroring that child back to himself or herself and accepting them as the complex, creative individuals that all children are.

She Taught Me about My Parents

It doesn't matter who my father was;
it matters who I remember he was.

—ANNE SEXTON, *A Small Journal*

As children, we see our parents as all-powerful, always in control. When these adults are overcome by illness or death, or are distracted by divorce, money issues, addictions, or other problems, children frequently feel that they are somehow at fault, and that their parents' unavailability is a reflection of how their parents feel about them. To make matters worse, children cannot talk to their parents about it because they are not there! Once again, aunties to the rescue. Our aunties can provide a perspective of our parents that can help us see them as not merely authoritarian figures, but also as humans who may be having a difficult time with issues that have nothing to do with how they feel about us. Lynn, a music producer in her forties, told us: "My brother tried for years and years to make it as a graphic artist and his five kids suffered from his intense focus on his career. His daughter, who married at eighteen, was still angry years later about how she didn't have her dad's attention during her childhood. About a year ago, we were talking about how she still resented him.

"I turned the conversation around to her adult married life situation. I could see on her face she had done something to really disappoint her husband. So, I asked her, 'What do you want to happen as a result of that situation?' And she said, 'I want him to forgive me.' And I said, 'Why would he forgive you?' And she said, 'Because he loves me.' And I asked, 'Why would he do that just because he loves you?' She just looked at me, speechless, and I said, 'You're in a situation where your dad did some things that you didn't like and you haven't forgiven him. Why would you expect forgiveness if you haven't extended forgiveness?'

"She got very quiet. The next day—I was so proud of her—she called her dad. Now they have an awesome relationship. He has been able to really encourage her and now they talk and act as the daddy and daughter they really wanted to be. An aunt gets to play a part that is so different than that of a parent or anyone else. As an aunt, I am heard by my nieces and nephews differently than they hear any other adult."

Lynn was able to help her niece understand how her father had made some mistakes, yet still loved his daughter. Aunties can provide support and healing not only when parents are distracted from their children, but also when a child begins to develop his or her independence. Children, at some point in their race to adulthood, start needing to establish themselves as adults, and desiring more equal footing with a parent. They may turn to an auntie not only to understand a parent better, but also to gain courage in achieving some autonomy. While an equal relationship between parent and child may never be fully possible, getting some insight and encouragement from an auntie about a parent may help give us the boost we need to start making some adjustments to the relationship.

Denise, a casting director, was touched when her niece contacted her to gain some insight about her mother, Denise's sister. Denise told us: "My niece grew up about two thousand miles from where I live. I'm not close to my sister, so I never saw them. Then about two years ago, one of my nieces got married. I went to the wedding with my son, who was then twenty and had not met any of his four cousins. Jennifer, the oldest, was in law school at the time. All the rest of them were in graduate school or college. I really enjoyed spending time with them. I noticed, even at that time, that Jennifer really reached out to me. She was also curious about her mother and what her mother used to be like. She wanted to put her mother in some kind of context."

When we asked how it felt to be put in that position with her own sister, whom she wasn't close to, Denise replied, "It's been very delicate, but I felt that Jennifer needed something from me, and I wanted to give it to her. She started to tell me more and more about my sister—she told me about all these difficult times she has had with her. I think it's really great for her to have someone who understands. I thought I was charting completely new territory as an aunt, but I guess my own aunts have played that same role for me, now that I think about it."

When we asked Denise if she could provide an example of how she helps her niece, she replied: "One day, Jennifer was telling me that she disagreed with her mother about how long her new baby should breastfeed. Jennifer said she couldn't argue back, that when my sister says anything to her, she doesn't ever speak back to her. But when *I* say something to Jennifer that she doesn't like, she immediately says,

'Why did you say that?'

"I said, 'Jennifer, you know how you can tell me what you think. You're able to stand up for yourself and speak up for what you want. If you can do it with me, why can't you do that with your mother?' So she said, 'I see what you mean. Maybe I could do that.' I try to help her put these kinds of things in perspective."

Although Denise was in her forties and Jennifer was in her twenties before they had any real contact, Denise feels an intimate bond with her niece: "I love her. She is really reaching out to me. She is so affectionate and outgoing and friendly and loving, it's like having a daughter. She's got this really sweet way about her and is very appreciative. I feel very maternal toward her."

Denise, and any other adult who is willing to step in and give a child guidance, takes the risk that the parent of the child may be offended or feel betrayed. As veteran auntie Ági wryly commented, "My sister to this day wants me to back her up on how she sees any problem with her children. Often I do, but sometimes I don't. That doesn't go over very well."

Nevertheless, even though it might not "go over very well," almost every auntie we spoke with felt that their loyalty was to the child and that they had to analyze each situation separately to determine the best course to take. Although difficult, if Denise can help Jennifer face her fear and understand and interact with her mother in an adult way, she will have contributed to all of their lives. Ultimately she will have fostered better communication between Jennifer and her mother, and gained the satisfaction of knowing she has helped Jennifer grow into a more mature, grounded adult.

Many individuals we interviewed talked about how their aunt formed a connection for them with a parent with whom they no longer lived or provided memories of a parent who had died. Aimee, a publicist now in her twenties, whose parents were divorced, missed seeing her father on a daily basis: "I was living with my mom. But being with my Aunt Beth, who was my father's only sister, made me feel connected to his family. She looked a lot like my dad, which made me feel close to him, even though I wasn't with him. He was remarried and I saw him on weekends, but I saw Beth during the week. There were no other nieces or nephews. So, I was the only child and the only niece. She was the only aunt. I was hers, kind of, and she was mine."

While Aimee was able to keep in contact with

her father through her aunt, her friend Elise, also in her twenties, told us about losing her father when she was thirteen: "My father had a chronic illness that was diagnosed when I was two. He then passed away when I was thirteen. He was sick my entire life. I was always asking relatives about my dad before he got sick to try to figure out who he was. My Aunt Alice has always been really good about talking to me about him. She tells me little stories she remembers—about my dad flying them around in his plane, or going sailing in San Diego, or about my dad's sense of humor, things like that. She talks to me a lot about when I was two or three and my mom got into a serious car accident and was in the hospital for a long time. My Aunt Alice is the one who came out and took care of me and my siblings. She tells me every now and then about how much she liked that and about the things that we did together."

Roxanne, a forty-five-year-old writer, remembers her Aunt Eileen being supportive of her when Roxanne's father was dying. Then, seventeen years later, when Roxanne had a book published, Aunt Eileen was the only one to remind Roxanne how her father would have felt about that accomplishment: "She said to me, 'Oh, your dad would be so proud of you.' It was really sweet but she is the only person who would ever say that to me. Her saying that meant she knew how close my dad and I were, and that he would have been really proud of me that I did that. And that was important to hear from her."

Gloria, now in her thirties, was able to learn more about her father after his death from his sister, her Auntie Eva: "I had only a little bit of contact with her as a child. My parents were divorced when I was young. She was always a lovely lady, but she never really figured much in my life. Then my father passed away when I was twenty-three. One of the only good things that came from that experience was getting to know my Auntie Eva and her husband, my Uncle Tom. She is a wonderful lady, now a huge role model and mentor in my life.

"I was very close to my dad, and I was racked with grief and pain from losing him. My Auntie Eva was so instrumental in my healing process, in my learning to deal with my dad's death. The way she did that so beautifully was just by spending lots of time with me. She let me share stories of my dad and she told me stories of her and my dad's childhood. I got to know my dad from a different perspective as I was also getting to know her.

"Shortly after my father passed away, she shared this story with me: My dad had this wood carving of a fish with a long pointed nose on his coffee table—it was his cherished piece of art. One time, my aunt and uncle and I were spending the night at Dad's house. In the evening, I accidentally snapped the nose off and was afraid to tell him. I scurried off to bed with the excuse that I was tired. Shortly after I had gone to sleep, my dad discovered the piece missing from his prize sculpture. He started to get very upset and asked my Auntie Eva what had happened. She said, 'Gloria did it by accident and didn't want you to know.' He immediately calmed down and said, 'Put it away. Don't say another word. I don't want her to feel bad about it.' If it had been anyone else there would have been severe punishment, but somehow I got away with breaking it. Not a word was spoken.

"She told me that story a couple of days after he died. Those stories were such a gift. Then, about three or four years ago, my aunt and uncle came up to stay with my husband, Steve, and me. We rented a movie in which there is a lovely tango scene. After the movie I commented that I would love to be able to dance like that. My Auntie Eva started recalling what a wonderful tango dancer my father was in high school.

She recounted her and my dad's experience with a high school ballroom dancing class and how he and this other gal would clear the floor when they danced.

"At first I was so shocked. My dad wasn't exactly a hip cat. It was kind of hard to imagine him as a dancer, and yet when she described it I saw a whole new side to him. I felt so grateful, because if it hadn't been for my Auntie Eva in my life, I never would have known that about my father. It really allowed me to see him differently.

"I am always grateful to be around Auntie Eva. I feel connected to my roots, to my heritage, when I am with her. She is the only living member of my dad's side of the family. She holds so much wonderful information, and I feel so lucky to have her."

Unless we have had the experience of losing a mother or father, we do not understand the longing for knowledge of that parent. Auntie Eva has shared herself with her niece, providing memories and history. In the process, she has allowed Gloria to see another side of her father, in a sense helping to keep him alive in her memory and alleviating her grief at losing him so young.

Wendy, the marketing director in her fifties who was taken care of as a small child by her Aunt Fern after her mother died, also was given much comfort by her Aunt Mabel: "My father and I always had a stormy relationship, but out of the blue I would hear from Aunt Mabel, who was my mother's oldest sister. She wasn't really an immediate part of the family, but she was able to talk to me about my mother and tell me stories about her, which was what I really wanted. When I was eighteen, she gave me some pictures of her. My father would never talk about my mother. When I was older, I somehow got the sense he did not want to upset my stepmother by remembering my mother. I now realize they probably never really knew each other all that well. It was wartime when they got married. He was away and then he was back. I was just a baby when she died.

"Aunt Mabel told me how much my mother loved me, in a number of different ways. She would say things like: 'When you were a baby your mother would never leave you—she always brought you with her.' I had always wanted to know what my mother was like. It turned out that Aunt Mabel could share with me that my mother had a terrific sense of humor, which was really nice. She also told me that my mother was a so-called bookworm, which is something that I have been accused of all my life. To find out that my mother had those same inclinations was a great comfort.

"She also talked about how much my grandfather disapproved of my father, but that my mother knew her own mind and if she wanted to do something it didn't matter who told her not to, she was going to do it. Everybody knew that about her. She had a strength of character, a certain resolve, a certain sense of herself. That made me feel good. Aunt Mabel also pointed out to me how much I looked like my mother. In an offhand way she told me that that's why my father sometimes had a hard time being around me. She helped me put it all in perspective and encouraged me to try to have this new life with my stepmother and father."

Aunt Mabel gave Wendy what she needed most as a young adult. Not only did she pass on the memories of Wendy's mother to her, but she helped her understand in a subtle way why her father may be hesitant to discuss Wendy's mother. By lifting the shroud of mystery that often settles around our parents, both living and dead, aunties may help us come to an understanding of our parents' demeanor, their actions, and their feelings about us.

We Have Such Fun Together

[P]lay is the "royal road" to the child's conscious and
unconscious inner world; if we want to understand
his inner world and help him with it,
we must learn to walk this road.

—BRUNO BETTELHEIM, *A Good Enough Parent*

"*I* always had fun with her." Many people we interviewed used these words or similar ones to describe their relationships with their aunties. Often our earliest memories include the sense that an auntie was one of the first people we loved to spend time with, the preferred adult playmate in our childhood. Because our exposure to aunts is usually somewhat limited, aunties can allow us more freedom. Unlike parents, who are primarily responsible for discipline in a child's life, aunties can be free to let children run a little wilder and can widen the boundaries of acceptable behavior.

Many aunties spoke of the joy in being able to be the "fun person" in a child's life, the one who allows just a little freedom from daily requirements at home. Carole, an executive, told us how she loves to visit her nephews and take them away from their parents for a while: "We wouldn't go as a whole family. I would go with just them, and we would do whatever they wanted. That could mean lunch at the local raucous pizza parlor, which my brother and Emily are so tired of they could scream. But I don't have to be begged to do this once a week. I am here only for a few days, so I can clearly tolerate a visit to the pizza place and get tremendous enjoyment out of it.

"Some of the pleasure is just the joy of being with them in a way that has nothing to do with discipline, although I won't take any crap from them. I always look at them and say, 'I don't have to do this. We are here because I want to be here, but when I ask you to do something, I expect you to do it.' The rules are very clear when we walk out the door and get in the car. They fight far less when they are with me than they do when they are clearly fighting for the attention of their parents. That relationship is totally different. They are sort of mine on a temporary basis.

"That's the one real thing about being an aunt versus having kids of your own. I have the luxury of doing only the fun stuff with them. I don't have to badger them into doing homework. I don't have to get them to pick up their rooms. I am the one who can say, 'Get your mitt and let's go outside and play baseball.'"

We found that aunties frequently let go of their own sense of decorum when around their nieces and nephews, as well. They willingly act silly for the amusement of a child and to allow that child to be silly too. Tessa told us about her Tante Annike ("Tante" is Dutch for "Aunt"): "For big entertainment, she would pull her teeth out. My grandma would just hate it when she did that, but she would do it when no one was looking. We would be sitting at the table and all of a sudden the teeth would come out, and then her whole face would be concave. Grandma would shout, 'Annike, put those teeth back in!' And my aunt would howl with laughter. She thought it was the finest thing to torture my poor grandma."

Aunties felt that having children in their lives helped them rediscover the joy of silliness, and gave them permission to experience the relief of pure fun, so often forgotten when we are adults. Carole told us about her niece Jacqueline: "I can say to her, 'Let's go outside and blow bubbles.' She loves it. We used to go stand outside and blow bubbles for about three hours. She would chase after them and pop them and want you to keep doing more. It just gives me a really carefree feeling, being outside and enjoying the beautiful weather. And also doing something that's making this small person giggle. There is just sheer joy all the way around. It's such a simple thing.

"It's only one dollar and fifty-nine cents for a little bottle of bubbles, but the kids are squealing and laughing and they could do it for hours. It just gives me the giggles to be out there watching them have such a good time, just from me blowing soap through a tiny hoop. I'll do it until eventually we will just fall over from exhaustion. But do you think I would go out in my own driveway as an adult and just blow bubbles? No, I wouldn't. But the action is totally justified by adding a two-year-old to that same scene."

Carole told us about another treasured moment with her niece Jacqueline: "My brother and the boys were outside playing baseball. She wasn't even two at the time—maybe she was between eighteen months and two years old. I was sitting on the driveway, and she sat down right next to me. I was leaning back on my hands. She leaned back on her hands. I had my legs stretched out straight onto the lawn and she stretched her legs out straight. I crossed my feet at the ankles and she crossed her feet at the ankles. It didn't take me long to figure out that she was mimicking everything that I was doing. So then I lifted up one hand to scratch my head and she lifted up one hand and fell over because she didn't have a good sense of balance yet.

"I started to giggle because I thought it was so funny. And I told my brother to watch. I uncrossed my legs and crossed them the other way. She uncrossed her legs and crossed them the other way. I tapped my feet and she tapped her feet. All of us got to laughing so hard, but she wasn't laughing. She didn't think there was anything funny about this because she was concentrating on doing exactly what I was doing. I don't know what made her do it. But all of a sudden she was sitting right next to me and thinking, 'I'm going to do what she does.' And that was very funny to watch and also a very sweet moment."

When aunties let down their serious adult guard, and engage in fanciful, silly, or other "childish" behavior, nieces and nephews are given permission to unleash their own playfulness and develop their own sense of humor. Eighteen-year-old Vanessa laughed as she recalled making jam with her honorary aunt, Kaki: "Kaki was the master sterilizer. She would boil the jars for the jam and use tongs so that no one could touch them. She used to make this really big melodramatic deal about sterilizing the jars—she'd yell, 'Don't touch the jars!' in a tongue-and-cheek way. I remember one time I was feeling very naughty while walking around the kitchen, and I came to the sterilized jars, all placed face down. Kaki was turned around, and I poked one of them. She didn't see me poke it, but she then saw the little fingerprint. She chased me around the house with the tongs, yelling 'You broke my jar, you broke my jar.' It was all so funny. She caught me, of course, and tackled me and pinched me very gently and playfully. She wrestled me to the ground with those tongs."

Erica, Vanessa's sister, described the fun she had baking with Sandy, Kaki's housemate: "The kitchen was huge, with a big oven in the middle. It took up about a third of the house. There was this ugly linoleum floor, white with specs of every color. There was a long countertop along one side. As I think back, I just have the sensation of flour everywhere, flour all over me, the counter, the floor. We had to knead the bread, and I remember standing on this stool, pulling the bread board out and piling a gargantuan mound of dough on it. I was little, and the whole thing was just immense. I am wearing this oversized apron, kneading the dough, then waiting and kneading it again, that is, until I got tired, then she kept kneading it. Then we finally baked it, and it smelled so good."

It is easy to imagine the lovely scene of these aunties taking the time to teach the girls their way around a kitchen while making the exercises playful and fun. Their attention supported these girls in the wake of their parents' divorce. They saw what it meant to be patient and creative and how to spend time with a good friend.

When parents divorce, both parents are grappling with the momentous changes going on in their own lives. Many times they are not in an emotional state to provide the fun every child needs. Other loving adults stepping in can make a significant difference in whether the divorce experience is unbearable for the children, or an experience from which the children can heal and survive. When Aimee's parents were divorced, she spent a lot of time with her Aunt Beth, whom she idolized with the intensity of a small girl: "My parents were divorced when I was two. My mom worked a lot, so I was frequently taken care of by the rest of the family. Aunt Beth was the only aunt who was around a good deal. She is only fifteen years older than me. I think that had a lot to do with why I thought she was so cool. Beth didn't have any sisters; and my mom and she just had a special relationship.

"I lived with my mom, but we didn't do fun things together. We did practical things. She was very busy. She was a nurse and worked twelve-hour shifts. She didn't have a whole lot of energy and was not very happy at that time. She made sure I did my homework or that I did the dishes. We got along fine, but she was my mom. But Beth wasn't. I think it was in fourth grade when she took me out of school for the day. My mom said it was okay. Beth took me ice-skating. We went to lunch. We went shopping. She also used to take me to Chicago on weekends to go to the museums and shopping. It was a big deal when I was little. She was cool—very fashionable and very beautiful."

Whatever it is, blowing bubbles till we drop from oxygen deprivation, ice-skating, or dropping our adult manner and engaging in downright undignified behavior, we can create those valuable connections with the children in our lives by doing the things for which their parents do not have either the time or the inclination. At any age, we bond with people with whom we can laugh and let down our guards. Through fun and silliness, we can accomplish the very serious goals of letting off steam and putting our problems in perspective, which refresh and prepare us for the more challenging aspects of our lives. Having fun with a child close to us can not only build their sense that life offers joy, but can also remind us aunties of that fact as well, all the while cementing the relationship between woman and child in a simple, loving way.

Many times our friends awaken another part of ourselves, a part we don't even know exists. We find ourselves attracted to someone who helps us unveil an aspect of our personalities we did not know we had or perhaps had not yet been ready to reveal. So it is with aunties. They can bring out a side of us that we may not share with our parents. Today a teacher, Barbara told us about how her auntie brought out her own playfulness and gave her the freedom to explore her development as a woman: "My mother was a very sweet, bright, serious lady. I never even told a joke or used bad language in front of her. There was a lot of respect and love and closeness. My mother and I had a lot of good, but serious, times together.

"But with my aunt I had fun—sheer pleasurable fun. It was just lively all the time. I wouldn't describe my mother as lively—she was too serious for that. She was the kind of person who took disappointments very hard, so I was always careful never to disappoint her. I guess in a sense I tried to be the perfect daughter for her. But when I visited my aunt, she and I lived it up. I went to parties and I don't remember ever going to church when I visited her. Auntie was always more like a girlfriend, a peer. I have great respect for her also. I can be myself with her, because I think all of that was part of me. At that time, I was serious on the one hand, this daughter of perfection, yet on the other hand I loved a good joke. A good laugh. A good party.

"My aunt had a lot of friends. She attracted both men and women. When she came to town, the house was always filled with her friends. And they were just so much fun. My mother's friends were social, but very quiet, subdued, well-mannered. They used to come over and we would just sit and talk. When my aunt's friends came over, we played cards, talked, laughed. My mother's friends would stay two to three hours, but my aunt's friends would be there from eight in the morning until eight that night."

If we wish to understand the puzzle that is us, all we have to do is look at the individual pieces—the people who formed us. Barbara, while a serious and conscientious girl, was able to develop another side of herself—the social, raucous, playful adult—through exposure to her aunt. Her auntie gave her the freedom to express herself, trusting that she was capable of taking care of herself. Similarly, Carole's sense of fun and liveliness is reactivated by her exposure to her nieces and nephews. If we are fortunate to have these aunties, nieces, and nephews, these friends who keep us attuned to the lighter side of life, we can readily see how they have helped form and exercise different parts of our personality and, most importantly, how they have kept us smiling.

My Good Friend

*A*s children, the first friendship we witness may be that between an auntie and our parents. Aunties' connections to parents help children see their parents in their roles as friends, and those connections can teach us about the importance and qualities of friendship. Erica told us about the central role her aunties' friendship to her mother played in her upbringing after her parents divorced: "An important thing about aunties is that you get to see your parents having friendships and relying on people. My sister and I had two single parents. Everyone knows being a single parent is really difficult. I know how hard my mom worked. I can't imagine that she could have lived through it without these other people. I really think of the aunt relationship as giving you a chance to see your parents be normal human beings. They need these other people, and you see them help each other out. They are role models not only in terms of who you are as a person, but also in terms of how to have good friendships."

Of course, not only does the auntie connection with our parents allow us to see friendship in action, but our aunties may be our first adult friends. Aimee found that the proximity in age and similar positions in their respective families brought her and her Aunt Beth together as pals and confidantes as well: "She smoked in front of me, but I couldn't tell Grandma. She would talk with her brothers in front of me, but she would do it differently in front of me than in front of an adult. She wasn't an adult. She was about twenty or twenty-two, but she was still Grandma's daughter and everybody else's little sister. Beth was one of the younger of the seven. She wasn't married. She had boyfriends. While she was older than me, she was still a kid as far as I could see. Within the family, she was the baby, and adored as the only girl child. I wasn't exactly a girlfriend, although I knew things about her that made me feel special for knowing."

In a sense, Aimee shared some of her aunt's life experiences, in that they were both young and each was the only girl in her immediate family. In essence, they grew up together, and their situation made them friends.

Even when not close in age, some aunties felt from the very beginning of a relationship with a small child that their connection was more about friend-ship than about mentoring or advice-giving. Many aunties find a budding new friend in a niece or nephew and enjoy the development and enduring nature of that friendship for the rest of their lives. Alta, now a ninety-two-year-old veteran fundraiser for the arts, talked about how she always viewed and treated her relationship with her grandniece Dale as a friendship: "I didn't treat her like a little girl. I never treat my friends as little children. I call them little people, but I always treat them like adults. I feel I can talk to them as if they're adults. Dale and I can go to lunch and talk about anything."

Similarly, Karen, an auntie to Lauren, now looks back at the time when she met Lauren, a young girl dealing with the difficulties of divorced parents, and sees how she was helped in her own maturing pro-cess by Lauren's example. She recalled: "My strongest impression from that time was just being amazed at the hard issues Lauren had to deal with. Lauren's father lived somewhere else and she lived with her mother and stepfather. Maybe the thing was that I was dealing with the same issues as an adult, making my own decisions about who I liked and who I cared about. I saw this girl have to make her own decisions about her father, knowing that her mother didn't like him. I watched this little girl deal with these big, big issues."

When we asked if Lauren's example helped Karen, who was Lauren's mother's best friend, she said, "I think that we all become more of the people that we are through the relationships that we have. So just watching her gave me insights about myself. I was introduced to her when she was a girl, but she was never a 'little' girl. She always was mature because she always had a big emotional load. I also love being around her relationship with her mother and being able to share in it because it is so special. Although now I feel like her surrogate mother, I didn't feel like that in the early years. I was just a friend."

Some women felt it was a matter of chemistry, that upon meeting a niece, nephew, or aunt, there was an immediate recognition and understanding of each other as a friend. Ági told us: "There is definitely chemistry. I have a special relationship with my niece Nikola. When she was a baby, I used to hold her and sing. She was hardly six months old, but there was something in her eyes, way before she could speak, that told me we shared so much. She was so rare. To this day she has a great sense of humor. She had it as a baby already—it was that sparkle in her eyes. There was this bonding—of humor and respect. There was immediate trust and love."

Whether a friendship is struck through a bolt of recognition or evolves as auntie and child share similar circumstances, these relationships are with us for life. As Ági told us when she described her friendship with another niece, Jessica, with whom she has always had a close friendship: "She was nine when I arrived in America. I was living in my sister's house for the first ten months, and I was pretty heartbroken because I had just left my husband. Jessica gave her room to me. That nine-year-old girl had so much compassion and respect. She would knock on the door of her room to retrieve some of her things and I would tell her she didn't have to knock on her own bedroom door. But she would say, 'Oh, yes I do, that's your room now.' She was always very lovely. We had the best times together."

Exterior circumstances have changed, but Ági finds their core connection is unaltered: "Now Jessica's thirty-seven. Of course our situations have changed—she is married and has her own child. But the basic relationship is still there. There is this open trust—trust, love, and appreciation. I feel that very strongly."

If life is especially good to us, as we become adults like Jessica we will be able to turn our relationships with our aunties into an adult friendship. We can still rely on their sage advice (who can't use plenty of that?) and continue to discuss our most personal concerns with a trusted auntie and friend. We, in turn, can become mentors, friends, and confidantes to the children in our lives, using what we have learned from some of the best teachers in our universe—our beloved aunties.

A Different Path

As time passes we all get better at blazing a trail
through the thicket of advice.

—ANNE McCAFFREY, *The Quotable Woman*

*L*ike Jimmy Stewart's character in *It's a Won-derful Life,* many of us have no idea how our lives affect the choices, attitudes, and paths of others. Many individuals we interviewed told us how an auntie provided a model for a different life path for them, how by watching their aunts they realized that there are choices in life besides those that their parents made. Connie, the journalist, told us how her aunt's decision to leave the Midwest decades ago has affected her and her entire family: "At the end of World War II, I was a small child growing up in the Missouri Ozarks. My very favorite aunt, who was my mother's much younger sister, went off to California to work after graduating from high school, which was very daring. I can't tell you how different that was at that time. She got on the Greyhound bus and left, which is the way midwestern people did it then.

"She was the true nonconformist of this family. Two of her friends had already moved to California.

At that time, California was so exotic, and she went there to work for American Airlines. That seemed very exotic too. She sent us wonderful gifts and wrote that she had been to premieres and seen movie stars. She worked part-time at a beautiful gift shop that movie stars frequented. This was my 'movie star' age too. She had been my favorite aunt in the Ozarks and I was brokenhearted when she left, but then delighted, because it was as if different worlds came into my life. Eventually several members of our family all ended up in California because of her. Her actions had a big influence on my life in ways that I was not even aware of at the time.

"My mother was the oldest of eight. She was very beautiful, but I don't think she ever had a lot of fun. This aunt, because she was in the middle—in fact, she is only about ten years older than me—always said that nobody paid any attention to her. She would wake up on that farm and think, 'What am I doing here? What should I do?' I think that what was different from most of my relatives was that she was a reflective person."

Connie followed her aunt to California, but much later. Nevertheless, we can see this wonderful image of her aunt getting on that Greyhound bus with Connie seated beside her in spirit. Connie recognizes the positive influence that her mother had on her as well: "It was a nice balance, I learned from both women." But Connie, who went to college and now lives in southern California, attributes her sense of the romantic and her sense of the possible, to her aunt's courageous choice to try something new: "My hometown isn't a place where most people stay. Most people did leave, but I think the romance—and I am an incurable romantic—was jumpstarted by that Greyhound bus trip to California."

In Connie's case, her favorite aunt introduced her to the exotic. Other women told us how their aunties introduced them to a more down-to-earth, less heady, existence. Goody, the hotel and coffee house owner, recalled how her aunts helped her appreciate the "Americana" point of view: "None of my mother's siblings had children. My mother didn't have us until she was in her forties, largely because of the Depression and because my parents were these socialist bohemian artists in Chicago who lived together without getting married, which in those days people didn't do very often. They really had an incredible decade in the thirties. My aunts didn't do that. They weren't part of these movements going on in the big city. Instead they were out in the country in a small town where they grew up teaching.

"Both of my aunts had college degrees. Even though they were extremely articulate and well read, however, they still held on to the traditional American dream, which my parents didn't do. I think the combination of both influences has been really healthy for me. Certainly I would not have wanted just the naive American dream. I give my parents the greatest credit for teaching me the most valuable lesson I could have learned, and that is, it's all in your curiosity. It's all in constantly learning and constantly being aware of and alert to the world around you.

"But my aunts added a lot of tenderness. They would read me sweet and romantic tales. My Aunt Helen loved animals. She would take a little bird in and watch it and take care of it. My Aunt Mary was that way about the children she taught in school. They became her whole world. I watched her total preoccupation with nurturing her school children. They were really more children-oriented than our parents were. I don't disregard for a moment that I think my father was the most wonderful person I have ever met. He was my companion and my mentor and the greatest source of joy of living I have ever had. But I still feel what I got from my aunts was a great connection with the rest of the world, with the simpler life."

As we talked about the African proverb "it takes an entire village to raise a child," Goody added: "I think that 'the village' allows you to acquire what you need to get along with all kinds of people and to not feel detached, not feel like a loner all the time. As alone as I can be sometimes, and I am alone a lot, I never feel alone because I have understood through my aunts that you really never are. It's simply all a matter of attitude, of how you look at it."

Many women who were influenced by their aunties, those older, cooler, wiser women, turned into older, cooler, wiser women who are there to help their nieces and nephews see alternative choices for their lives. Rhett, born in a small town in the South and now living in California, was provided a model for her current life that she is now passing on to her nieces: "I grew up in a small town. My family had been there for generations. No one ever left. They just stayed there and took over their fathers' businesses. My mother had a best friend who moved to San Francisco (which I thought was really glamorous), and was an interior designer. She would send me neat things from San Francisco. This was during the Summer of Love, and she sent me psychedelic posters from the Haight-Ashbury district, trinkets from Chinatown, stylish, unusual things that had never seen the light of day in my hometown. To a girl in the South, this was a very different world. In many ways, she was my ticket out."

Now Rhett provides a different model to her own nieces: "I think we can be insulated in our family of origin. Part of the whole process of growing up and maturing is separating from that family, and aunties can help us do that. I chose not to have children of my own, and what I have to offer kids is different from what somebody who has chosen to be a traditional wife and mother can give. Parents are so busy, and their focus is so different. My brother's wife, who was married in her early twenties and has been raising a family, told me: 'I want them to get your perspective. Your life is so different from our life, and I think that it is important that they make up their own minds about how they want to live. They can choose when they get old enough what they really want.' Aunties have always helped children separate from their parents."

Robin, the psychologist and a minister, took great

joy and delight in modeling to her nieces (and nephews!) that women can be or do anything. "My brother is the nurse and I am the minister in the family. Between Aunt Robin, who is also Reverend Robin Williams, and Uncle Jimmie, who served as a nurse in the MASH unit in Korea and is currently a nurse in a prison facility in the Midwest, my nieces and nephews understand that men and women can invest their lives in ways that really work with their passions and their gifts, regardless of traditional gender roles.

"When she was about three years old, one of my nieces announced that she was going to be a nurse when she grew up. I looked at her encouragingly and brightly responded, 'Or maybe a doctor?' She looked at me for a moment and then decidedly said, 'Well, probably a nurse.' I admit I longed for her to be the new Surgeon General, but I decided that day I had better be sure that I didn't impose Aunt Robin's agenda on her! I did strive both by example of my own less-than-traditional life as a female clergy as well as in conversations together to always remind my nieces and nephews that they could do or be anything they wanted. At one point I purchased a whole line of large children's story books which chronicled the lives of women who had made a huge impact on society. Those books told the stories in pictures and large print of the first woman social worker in America, the first woman doctor, the first woman to own and run a newspaper, and so forth.

"I was delighted recently when my now married second-born niece asked me where those books are because she wants to have them someday for her own children!"

Actions indeed do speak louder than words, and illustrating principles by example probably has the most powerful influence on children. When the children were younger, Robin would take them with her to her office. "I was a pastor and a denominational executive at that time. If I was preaching on a Sunday, I would take them with me. They would be in the congregation and they would go out with the resident pastor and me for a meal after the service. I took them to Europe when I was preaching over there, and I liked the fact that they got to see me in that role. They saw that women could be ministers and pastors, that women could speak in front of crowds of people and that it was a very appropriate role."

Parents seem to feel a lot of guilt these days. Because there is an increasing awareness of the psychological effects that parents' actions have on children, mothers and fathers may cringe at every mistake they make with their sons and daughters. But they can take some of the heat off themselves when they realize that they are not the only ones who influence us when we are growing up.

Aunties add a whole new dimension to children's lives, and parents who wish their children to see what the world can offer them not only provide the richness of their own experience but also the experiences of their siblings and trusted friends. Some parents perhaps would not choose that their children follow in the footsteps of their aunties. For instance, a more "traditional" set of parents may wish their daughter to marry and live a conservative lifestyle, and parents who consider themselves "liberal" may be horrified at the choice of a child to follow a conservative path. No one has ever denied that it is a parent's right—or duty—to worry about their children's choices. We give credit to those parents who overcome their fears, trust their sisters, and rely on their children to do the right thing for themselves.

She's on My Side

What do we live for, if it is not to make life less difficult for each other?

—GEORGE ELIOT, *The Quotable Woman*

*O*ur aunties not only illustrate alternative life paths to nieces and nephews, but through their position as "inside outsiders," they also help family members understand and appreciate one another. Aunties hold a unique position—that of being trusted family or "adopted" family members, who nevertheless have a little distance on the relationship between parents and children, and thus are able to see all of the family members as individuals.

Eliza, an attorney who grew up in the South, recalled that her three aunts subtly provided for Eliza's parents a different perspective on the value of their children's accomplishments and talents: "My aunts were very respectful of my parents and urged me to be, but they would express their excitement about good grades or something I had done, an achievement they would then make clear to my parents was outside the norm. It was very subtle. My parents' attitude toward grades was sort of, 'You got

127

an A, that's great,' and they would throw the report card aside. But my aunts were very supportive of school achievements.

"They were also champions for my brother in terms of his art. They felt very strongly that he should have private lessons. It was not that my parents opposed it—they just didn't have any particular interest in following it. They felt he should get his training at school. So my aunts were more advocates by example, by doing things separately with us and making clear that they were proud of us."

Aunties frequently see their role as being the advocate for the child, as keeping their eye on the child's welfare, even at the risk of alienating the child's parents. Eliza's aunts showed their support subtly, but sometimes circumstances and personalities force that partisanship into the open. Tessa took that risk with her niece when she supported her running away from home, because she felt that ultimately it was the best way to give the child a safe way to return: "My brother's daughter, Aja, was born when he was twenty or twenty-one. All of a sudden he had this daughter, and by the time she was twelve, he started setting down these rules for her because he realized he was a parent. And I didn't understand because I knew him as my brother, and all of a sudden he was concerned about whether she was wearing makeup to school and those sorts of things. As her aunt, I don't worry about that sort of everyday detail.

"She was going to run away from home when she was sixteen and she didn't have any money. I knew she was going to go no matter what. She wanted to quit school, so she called me and asked if she could talk to me. I said, 'Of course.' Then she asked me for money. As her friend, I didn't want to see her getting into any more trouble than she was already going to get into, and I thought, 'Well, she is going to run away anyway.' So rather than have her on the street, I decided to give her the money. But then as her aunt, I said, 'Aja, this is not the way. I have to say this to you as your aunt. If I was your parent I'd say the same thing. This isn't the way I would want you to do things. But I am going to give the money to you because I know you're going to do it and I don't want you to think you are alone.' Giving the money to her created havoc in my family. My brother was livid with me. He thought that I wasn't playing my aunt role properly. He thought my role was to be on his side and to act as though I were her parent. He thought I had gotten confused somewhere along the line."

Because giving Aja the money seemed like such a risky thing to do, both with respect to Aja's safety and to Tessa's relationship with her brother, we wondered if Tessa regretted helping Aja in that way. She replied: "No. I think I was having to make a choice between my brother, whom I adore, and my niece. I knew he was having a lot of problems with her at the time, but you have to do what you think is best for that person. I wasn't worried about him. He had a house and a job and his wife and other children. I was worried about her and the fact that she was sixteen and going to hitchhike to Montreal with no money. I could talk to her until I was blue in the face, but I didn't think it was my position to do so at that point. I pointed out to her everything that I was thinking and then stood aside and said, 'Good luck, this is what I can give you. If you need to call, you can always call collect.'

"She went to Montreal and stayed with a friend there, and eventually she came back. She was okay and moved back home again. Then they went through the whole thing again, and she moved out again. They went through a lot. Now they have a good relationship."

While some of us may not feel comfortable with

Tessa's actions, it turned out that her niece was able to stay connected with her family through her. Another woman, Jennifer, a forty-one-year-old marketing assistant, whom we were interviewing at the same time as we interviewed Tessa, supported Tessa's actions: "I would have done the same thing. If something happened or became difficult and she wanted to come back, then she would have someone whom she felt she could contact and come back to. She didn't have to feel that she was out there alone, that everyone hated her, and that she had no means of getting back."

Jennifer continued by describing her support of her own niece, Dionne, when Dionne was trying to find her way as a young adult: "I was always considered to be the rebellious one in my family because I always questioned everything. I saw that Dionne, my oldest niece, was going to be exactly the same way. I remember not having anyone that I could confide in when I was that age. I felt that she and I had a relationship of trust when she was growing up, that when she felt times were difficult, she could always talk to me. I'm like Tessa. There were times when I didn't always agree with the things Dionne wanted to do, but I supported her and respected the fact that she was twenty years old and could make those decisions. I got married when I was twenty-three. In the big scheme of things, the age difference between me then and Dionne now wasn't that big. I found it amazing that her mother could be so strict with her when she herself got married at nineteen. Yet the thought of Dionne moving in with a group of girls and sharing a house was such an appalling thought to her. I said, 'Hold on just a minute. You were married at nineteen and I was married at twenty-three. I left home at nineteen and got a place of my own.'"

An auntie's job is to see her niece or nephew as a growing adult, not as someone who is going to remain small forever, a position that parents can sometimes take. Nevertheless, Tessa realizes that parents have a difficult task, and she is sympathetic to their responsibilities. Tessa acknowledged that she may not have taken the same position if Aja had been her daughter instead of her niece: "I don't have any children, and if I had a daughter who was sixteen and wanted to run away, I don't know if I would hand her the money and say, 'You need to go and do what you need to do.' I don't know that as a parent I could do that easily, but as an aunt I could."

What was indicated in all our interviews with

women who had beloved aunties was that they knew their parents were doing the best they could. Parents are trying to compensate for what they perceive to be unhealthy about their own upbringing and to help their kids avoid the pitfalls of growing up. But nobody does it perfectly, and we are very lucky if we have other loving adults in our lives to voluntarily present our case, to be on our side when it seems that no other adult is.

A parent's positive attitude toward the aunt relationship can make that relationship stronger. And parents can anticipate the inevitable occurrence of a clash between them and their child and enlist an aunt's help now. Rosalyn, the producer, told us how her sister-in-law prepared for the moment of teenage rebellion and looked to her for backup: "My relationship with my niece has really been helped by her parents' attitude. When she was about five, her mother looked at me and said, 'You know, when she gets to be sixteen, she is going to run away from home. Anything I can do now to make sure she runs to your house, I really want to do.' That's been key. They are incredible parents and have been extremely generous in terms of their not only allowing, but also supporting, the relationship."

Sometimes aunts can advocate subtly, by emphasizing a child's accomplishments and talents and encouraging a parent to do the same. Other times, such as in the case of Tessa and her niece Aja, being a child's advocate requires an even stronger stand, one that puts the relationship with the parents at risk. Being an advocate for the child, of course, does not require that an auntie always support a child's point of view. Our job as aunties is to decide for ourselves what will be most beneficial for the child over the long term and to take the action that we believe is in that child's best interest. Tessa did not believe that Aja was doing the right thing by running away from home. She could have just as easily, and just as legitimately in her role of aunt, decided that she would not give her niece the money. The point is that Tessa did what she thought was best, and no one can ask for more from anyone. No parent can be everything to their child and it can sometimes be impossible to discipline and support a child simultaneously. But with a few extra caring adults like aunties, kids can come close to "having it all."

I Can Talk to Her about Anything

[T]he cornerstone of the love that nurtures
is psychological safety.

—DOROTHY CORKILLE BRIGGS, *Your Child's Self-Esteem*

One of the most important functions that aunts serve is providing a sympathetic ear. Frequently we were told that aunties can listen without judging, especially when going through the difficulty of adolescence. Many women told us that they felt welcome to talk to aunties about matters they may feel uncomfortable talking about with their parents, teachers, or other adults in authoritative positions. Cindy, a librarian now in her thirties, told us how her aunt was able to hear and talk about the thorny issue of sex when Cindy was thirteen years old: "I talked to Aunt Betsy about my girlfriend whom I was having trouble with at the time. One of my best friends from fourth grade, Renee, had sex when she was thirteen. That really made me uncomfortable. I talked to Betsy about it, because I was freaked out.

"My grandma lived in this beautiful house in which all her children grew up. I was sitting at the top of the stairs, to be away from everything and everyone that was downstairs. I had Betsy on the phone. I was uncomfortable and saying I didn't know what to do. Renee had lost her virginity, and it was nothing like the storybook scenario I had hoped for. She was thirteen, and she was drunk. She left his house alone and rode home on her bike. I was mad at her for doing this to herself.

"So Betsy talked to me about her best friend when she was very young. She said, 'When I was in high school, she was always a little bit "faster" than I was, and all these people paid more attention to her than to me.' She used her own story to make me feel a little more comfortable. She didn't judge. She reacted to what I was saying, but her reaction wasn't 'Don't hang out with her anymore.' My mom would have gotten angry. Betsy could deal with it on a more reasonable level. She didn't have to protect me from anything."

As we grow up, talking to an adult we trust about adult matters can provide comfort as well as confirmation that we are taking the correct steps in our lives. Susan, a thirty-seven-year-old flight attendant, whose Aunt Kae played a crucial role in Susan's upbringing, continues to look to her aunt for guidance and comfort. She told us, "When my parents divorced, I lived with my mother, but I spent every weekend and most summers with my Aunt Kae, all the way up to when I was fifteen or sixteen. When my mom had to move to a bad part of town, which was all she could afford, my Aunt Kae picked me up every day for school for a year so I could go to a better school in another neighborhood. She provided the stability I needed then and continues to show me unconditional love.

"I still rely on her. She is the first person I call when I am in trouble or someone in my family is in trouble, and when I am sad or upset in any way. She always comes through for me, and helps me work through my problems. My aunt has made all the difference in my life. Her love has meant more to me than anything."

Marie, a hairdresser, finds that her rich auntie relationships not only let her share the tough discussions about external things going on in her life, but also allow her and her aunts to express their anger or disappointment with each other. "With my aunts, I have a very honest relationship. My aunts and I have relationships in which if something is wrong we will say it. I remember having fights with my aunts. Once I forgot my Aunt Ruth's birthday.

She was very annoyed. She called me up and let me have it: 'I can't believe you forgot my birthday.' She was not teasing, she was really hurt and upset, and it was terrifying. She was really angry and let me know that I had done something that was really uncaring and she didn't like it. I apologized, and I haven't forgotten her birthday since."

Learning to be honest and open with another person better prepares us for any relationship we have in our lives, whether it's with our spouses, our friends, or our children. Additionally, we all need to learn how to listen. Many aunties understand the importance of their role as noncritical listeners, and find themselves checking their own desires to give advice. Linda told us about a young child to whom she is an auntie: "He was telling me how he was having trouble with bullies in the neighborhood, and how there was a family discussion about it. Later, he and I were alone, and I said that his experience sounded really horrible. He said, 'Yes, it is.' I asked him what he was going to do about it. He told me all the good advice he had gotten from other adults.

"I asked him what he was going to do. He said, 'I don't know.' I asked if he thought any of the solutions that were suggested were going to work, and he said, 'No, I don't.' So I asked him what he thought would happen. He said, 'Well, I guess we'll just get older and get used to each other.'

"I thought it was really great that he could see into the future, when things would be better, that it wouldn't always be this way. I have to restrain myself sometimes, because every adult wants to tell kids how it really is. I told him I have been bullied and picked on too, and that it was really hard and bothered me a lot, but that he was right: 'It won't always be this way, you'll get older, they'll move away, something will happen. You can't let it ruin your life or let it get you down too much. It will be all right.'

"I think lots of times when children start to tell their problems to adults, the adults are too quick to try to get in there and fix everything. I just try to really listen. The more you don't come back with ten thousand solutions, the more they talk and you find out what really is going on. Lots of times the first thing they come out with is not the thing that is truly bothering them."

Once a child gains confidence that she or he is free to talk to an auntie without being judged or criticized, then auntie and child can share both the celebratory and the difficult times. As a child grows, their problems and choices become more complex. Jennifer told us that her nieces keep her informed about their most personal decisions as they grow into young women: "They like the fact they can talk to me about anything within reason, although we have worked very hard to keep that fine line of respect. They never forget that I am their aunt and that I'm older. That traditional aspect of our relationship is still there. But any time they have difficulties or problems, their mothers always know that at some point if they can't get to the problem, I will find out about it from the girls' letters to me.

"They tell me all their horror stories. I was really sort of pleased that my niece, Melissa, the second oldest one, who I thought was going to have a lot of difficulties with men because her parents had a very messy divorce, told me about her first sexual experience. She said it was wonderful. She must have happened to find the one boy of her age who was romantic. He had candles and music and he had taken her out to dinner. He really wooed her. She was eighteen years old and had been with this guy for a year. She had made the decision that she wanted to have her first sexual experience with him. And she wrote to me saying she was thinking about it.

She never told me when it happened, but when she told me about it, I was really pleased for her."

When we asked whether Melissa had shared any of that experience with her mother and father, Jennifer replied, "No. I know that Melissa's mother lived in a little fantasy world that her daughter was still a virgin until she was at least twenty-two. With my sister, that was the best way to keep it. She would have flipped. When I get together with my sisters and talk about their children, it surprises me to see their expectations of their children and their view of who their children really are. I feel that my oldest sister especially is missing out on this wonderful child, Dionne, whom she doesn't really know. I think that is sad. She has this really intelligent twenty-year-old, a really vibrant girl who is completely different in her mother's company because of her mother's expectations of her."

Even when our parents may welcome our confidences, we may not be ready to share every feeling with them. Vanessa told us how her honorary aunt, Sandy, helped her when her first love moved away: "My family and Sandy and I were on a camping trip together. My boyfriend of two years had just left for college, moving to another state. I was not in a good place at all. I cried every day and was very irritable. I could not function normally. As a result, I was having a lot of tension with my mother and stepfather. They were very concerned—they love us girls a lot. They were worried because I was so sad and not eating. But at that point, I just didn't want the attention at all. I didn't want anyone asking, 'How are you doing? Can we do anything for you?' I don't remember if I was really rude to them; I probably was. But I remember feeling really angry that my space was being invaded and wondering why they couldn't just let me grieve by myself.

"I was on this camping trip and I didn't have any of my friends to go to, just all these adults. Sandy came to me either the third or fourth morning of the trip and said, 'I want to go for a hike, and I think that you should come with me.' So we went. She said, 'I know that you are having trouble with Scott leaving. I know that you must be in an incredible place of grief. I want you to know that I understand why you might be having this trouble with your parents. They are concerned about you, and they seem intrusive. I understand that it might be really hard for you. They want to do what is best for you but they don't really know what to do for you right now. I don't think that they understood how much you loved this person until you lost him.'

"I said, 'Yeah, I know, they just want what is best for me. I know they love me, but they are so annoying. At this point I am so irritated with them.' Sandy not only tried to help me deal with why was I feeling all this anger toward my parents, but she also helped me channel some of it. She suggested that I direct some anger toward a more constructive goal, such as going on a long hike. She helped me get rid of a lot of energy. She didn't try to convince me that I was treating them badly or that I needed to stop. She didn't try to change my behavior at all, but she did help me understand that I just needed to be patient with myself and with my parents.

"I doubt that my mom put her up to it. That is not the kind of thing that our family does at all. I know that Sandy just saw what was going on and knew that I needed some help. She offered to be there for me after the camping trip as well. She made sure that I understood that I could call her any time I needed. It was a great resource to have, when I wanted to be able to confide in my mother and felt like I couldn't. She saved us all a lot of pain. Having an outside source, an objective observer, really helped."

Undoubtedly, Vanessa's mother was relieved to know that Vanessa had someone to go to with her heartache. In her book *Cherishing Our Daughters,* Dr. Bassoff, also a mother, discusses her own sense of relief, although mixed with a little jealousy, when her adolescent daughter went to other adults to discuss delicate matters: "When Leah as an adolescent found it difficult to talk about personal matters with me, she sought out adult female confidantes and became especially attached to two of her acting teachers, Melody and Betty. Whenever I began feeling envious of these women for being an intimate part of my daughter's life in a way that I was not, I forced myself to recognize the great service they were performing for her. Mature and wise, they counseled her in matters of love and sex, sensitively preparing her for womanhood. I recall one incident in particular: It was my turn to pick up Leah and her friends from acting class and drive them home. Arriving a bit early, I took a seat at the back of the darkened auditorium, where a rehearsal was in progress. Unobserved, I watched Melody confidently guide my inexperienced daughter through a tender kissing scene with a young, similarly inexperienced male actor."[14]

Ultimately, young adults need the input of other

adults. Tessa told us what she tried to accomplish with her niece when she was growing up: "I was thinking about what I would want to be for my nieces and nephews. I want to be someone who uses my life experience to allow me to accept them for who they are. Rather than projecting all my experience onto them, I can use that experience to be open enough all the time, no matter what they throw at me, to be able to talk to them about it and be there unconditionally. I think that is the most important thing."

We agree. Think about how much pain and uncertainty everyone could be spared if each of us had an older, more experienced adult to whom we could talk when we were growing up, an adult who listened without judgment and who understood that we were human beings who had problems and made mistakes just like everyone else. Such sympathetic ears are invaluable.

Keeping Secrets

I feel honored and have a new sense of responsibility
when my niece shares things with me
she's not ready to tell anyone else.

—PAMELA SCHRAEDER, contributor

*W*hen a child trusts an auntie enough to share a confidence with her, how much should an aunt respect that confidence? An auntie is close to the child and is usually close to the parents as well. As aunties, when we find out information that would be troubling to a parent, to whom are we loyal?

Some aunties feel that the trust the parents put in them requires that they share what is going on with the child. Marilou, a thirty-year-old accounting clerk, told us: "I haven't yet needed to be an advocate for a niece or nephew. But I am afraid I am going to have to do that with Ashley when she reaches her teenage years. We have even talked about it. Ashley and I are really close. She may ask me or tell me something that I feel I have to tell her mother, because she needs to know. I think if it were a major issue I would have to do so. But if I tell, I would be betraying Ashley's trust in me. Then I think Ashley would never forgive me. Right now, I just hope there's nothing major that I would feel obliged to tell Lisa."

Marilou's sister, Rose, has a similiar ambivalence about revealing a confidence: "Our other niece Katrina opened up to me about something she was feeling very deeply. She was maybe five at the time. We were alone watching TV and all of a sudden she just started blurting out all these deep feelings she has about stuff that was bothering her. I didn't know what to say. These were things that were really important to her. Then I said something to her mother, Lisa, about it and she said that Katrina didn't talk about that kind of thing to her. I thought, 'Should I have said something to Lisa?' and then I thought, 'What if she tells her secrets to me when she's older? What will I say?' I could just picture her saying, 'Promise me you won't tell my mommy.' I don't know if I could do that, but I would probably go so far as to say, 'If you need me to be there with you then I will be there,' so they don't feel so alone."

Like Marilou and Rose, most of the aunties to whom we spoke felt that they could not give an absolute answer to the issue of confidentiality. Instead, most felt they would have to weigh the interests of the child against the interests of the parent in each situation. Although Wendy, in her fifties, has yet to make a big decision of this sort with respect to her niece, she feels that it's important to be sympathetic to both interests: "I have never been put into a position in which I have had to decide whether I should betray her confidence to her folks. That might happen later on. She is only nine, but I think that I would try to decide what I felt was the best overall for her.

"If I could handle the problem without the parents' input, and thought that the right thing was going to happen and that I could help the child face up to whatever she needed to do, then maybe I wouldn't tell them. I'm not sure exactly what the situation would be, but if it seemed that it would be best for the parents to be involved, then of course I would try to involve them. The truth is you are not the child's parent. One of the best things you can do for the child is to have a certain point of empathy with the parent, even if your views are different."

When we asked her to explain what she meant, she said, "I just think in most cases the child isn't your child and isn't going to come and live with you. You are not going to be able to manage that child's whole world. The parents are doing that. So you have to have some kind of empathy with the parents; on some level you need to see their point of view. The best way to help the child with certain situations is to help the parents see things differently. You can't just remove the child from that situation. They are in it and they are generally not in control."

Deborah, the program manager, also found that involving the parents in a child's confidence may not constitute a betrayal: "I'm trying to maintain contact with the kids and be a solid grounding place. I know that the storminess of adolescence is going to hit these kids soon. I have told them several different times that I know there may be times when they don't feel comfortable talking about something with their parents. I tell them, 'I want you to remember that you can always call me. I want you to know if you feel sad or scared or lonesome and you don't have anyone you want to talk with, you can call me.' I think kids need that reassurance that there really is a lifeline someplace when they face the challenges that they face.

"I remember having a conversation with the two older boys about a year ago in which I asked them if they knew what it meant to honor a confidence. They weren't really sure what that meant, so I explained it to them. I told them that if anything ever comes up that they really cannot talk about with their parents or their teachers, and that if they talked about it with me, I would not betray their confidence. If it turned out that there were big things, I said that I would at least tell them when we needed to talk to another grownup as well. I told them I wouldn't do anything like that behind their backs. They understood, and I think that's part of the trust that we feel mutually."

Children do understand. When they trust us enough to tell us something in confidence, they also trust us enough to decide when other people need to get involved. Olivia, who is now in her forties and just lost her beloved aunt, had that overall trust in her aunt's judgment: "I don't feel that I ever spoke in confidence and had that confidence betrayed. Absolutely not. There may have been some time when I talked to her and she talked to my mother. But I can't even conceive of her betraying me. There was such a level of trust that I felt like if she felt it was right to betray that secret, then go on, girl. It's just unquestionable."

Olivia and her aunt also found a way to talk about personal issues that never forced her aunt to decide whether she must betray a confidence of Olivia's:

"There were some things that I talked about with my aunt more than with my mother. But regarding the most personal decisions for me, the most difficult, I talked around them with her. She would never pry or say, 'Are we talking about you?' There was just a real sensitivity there, so we could talk. I am thinking in particular about an abortion I had and I couldn't talk even to her. But somehow I think she sensed what was going on with me and she basically said that she was accepting of that decision in a woman's life. I think she knew."

Keeping confidences goes both ways. Linda, the corporate executive, sees a duty not only to earn the trust of a child, but also to act as a confidante for the parents. By relieving a parent's concern, an auntie can help take the pressure off both parent and child. Unburdened parents may, in turn, be more relaxed with their children. As Linda explained: "Sometimes I am a sounding board for the parent. I feel like I am much closer to my friends for whom I am god-mother to their children because they selected me to have a special interest in their child, and I do. Therefore, I am a confidante for the parent as well. I know that those parents tell me their fears and concerns, maybe even about inadequacies in their children, and they wouldn't express these things to just anyone. They can tell me because they know I have a particular relationship with, and interest in, this child as well. I always try to be completely nurturing to the parent too."

Charity begins at home, in our inner circle. If we as aunties can extend a nonjudgmental ear, a loving heart, and a place of comfort to the children (and parents) we love, whether they are related to us or not, we can do those children a great service. And parents are grateful. As Marilou said about her son Vincent going to his aunts for advice, or just a listening ear, when he gets older: "I hope if Vincent feels uncomfortable talking to me about something, that he will go to his aunts to talk, instead of going to another adult he doesn't know very well. They will give him trusted advice, good advice. I won't have to worry about it." The generosity aunties show in this regard will be their contribution to bringing up a secure next generation of humans and a more relaxed set of parents.

My Auntie Always Knows
What I Want

It is better to give and receive.

—BERNARD GUNTHER, *Sunbeams*

hat do we look forward to most as children? Presents! Many women we interviewed came to associate a certain gift with a particular auntie, something they could look forward to every year. Ellen, an executive assistant in her thirties, told us about her Great Aunt Betty, "the aunt from California who always sent cases of large oranges and grapefruits at Christmas. And when she visited us, she always brought all this fruit. She would even bring strawberries! When I was a child living in the Midwest, it was amazing to get fruit like that in the middle of winter."

Similarly, Sarah, now thirty-five years old, continues to receive every year a birthday card with ten dollars and glitter inside from her Aunt Lenore. "When I was little, it was unbelievably exciting. And now that I am big it is hysterical—not only because it is predictable, and because now ten dollars has a completely different impact, but because it is so indicative of her personality. The glitter is just so Aunt Lenore, so glamorous. When I was in college, and everybody was wearing thrift-store party dresses, she gave me a green chiffon dress and an orange chiffon dress that were to die for. She has also given me beaded sweaters. She had fashion going when it counted."

These kinds of presents become part of a tradition in themselves and may be valued for how reflective they are of the person giving the gift. But some people we interviewed told us about gifts from aunties that were simply thoughtful and delightful in themselves. We often heard the phrase, "She gave me the most beautiful. . . ." Many remembered quite clearly the gifts that their aunties had given them when they were growing up and talked with delight about their own efforts to give the special children in their lives the perfect gift.

Linda expressed her pleasure in giving when she talked about the gift that she had made for her god-daughter Katie: "When they are very small I am the fairy godmother. I give them the most outrageous gifts I can think of, the dream gifts. Whatever it is they have conjured up in their minds—or whatever I think they really want and don't imagine that they'll get—that's what I find for them. An example is the pink teepee that I had made for Katie when she was younger.

"Katie is an Indian Princess, which is a father-daughter club. She was seven at the time. I wasn't sure she actually wanted a teepee, but I felt that it would be a perfect metaphor for her at that age. She needed a fort of her own, where her little brother couldn't come, and that would clearly be a girls' fort and not a boys' fort. I had already gotten her a few Indian Princess theme gifts that had gone over very well, so I decided for her seventh birthday that a teepee would be a great gift. I had her name embroidered on it. There were beads all over it. It was beautiful, all hand done.

"As always, I went over and helped with her birthday party. Her dad and I set up the teepee in this little glade, and we put all the presents from the other guests inside it. When it was time to open the presents, we blindfolded her and led her to the glade. When we took her blindfold off, it was beyond my wildest hopes. Her mouth was hanging open, her eyes were wide as saucers. She was just thrilled.

"Katie knew immediately who it was from, and she turned to me and said, 'Auntie Linda, thank you for the teepee.' I asked her how she knew. She said, 'You are the only one who would think of giving me a teepee.' I was tremendously gratified by that. She was really excited about it. It was the perfect gift."

Can you imagine? We wanted Linda to be our auntie! *We* want a pink teepee too! But why such an extravagant gift? We knew that Katie was thrilled by the gift, but why did Linda seem just as excited when she was telling us about it? When we asked Linda why she thought it was important to give a child an ideal present and how she was so inspired, she said, "I think your parents often give you great gifts, but parents also have a practical bent. At one point, my friend Lori suggested that I get Katie some summer clothes. I said, 'I'm sorry—I will buy her summer clothes, but don't you dare tell her that I bought them.' I don't want her to associate me with anything practical in that way. I want her to think of me as someone who finds the perfect thing, not someone who buys socks.

"I was lucky because I had a special person in my life who was like this, who had this almost divine sense of exactly the right gift for me. Aunt Marguerite was an honorary aunt, not a godmother, but I am still very close to her. She just took me on. We met when I was about two. She always came up with the perfect gift, and she would wrap it so elaborately that it would be almost too beautiful to open.

"When I got those gifts, I felt really special. Somebody who was not my parent, not obligated to care, really cared about me and made me feel really great. I was fascinated that this adult would take time out of her own life to care one way or the other about what I might want. When it was so clear that she had put a lot of energy and expense into something, I was flattered and amazed and grateful and appreciative.

"My parents didn't have very much money, so Aunt Marguerite bought me a ruby ring for my thirteenth birthday, because she thought that birthday was a big deal. My parents could never have afforded it. She bought me this beautiful, yet modest, ruby ring, very tasteful. I thought I had died and gone to heaven. Part of it was the way she would bestow a gift, it was almost ceremonial—it was like she was saying, 'Well, you are a young lady now.' Aunt Marguerite was telling me with her gift that I had 'arrived' and that it was time to have some nicer jewelry. I was just astounded."

Linda continued, "She bought me real pearls when I turned sixteen. She explained how to take care of them, what the right length is to start with, and so on. We picked out the 'starter' pearls together. It was very nice. I didn't think she should be spending this much money, and I was trying to select the cheapest pearls. Simultaneously, of course, she was busy trying to talk to me about the pearls I should have—'You are going to have these the rest of your life,' and so forth. I said, 'They are going to cost you so much money,' and she said, 'You should not be concerned about that. I have been saving up for these for a long time now and all these pearls are within the budget.' Little did I know—and I didn't find this out until later—she had already been to the store and had picked out an array of things for the jeweler to show me, thereby cleverly managing her own expense. She didn't let them bring out the twelve-hundred-dollar freshwater pearls. She had them bring out eight sets, each a little different. When we were done choosing, the jeweler gave me a beautiful velvet box with my pearls in them. It was such a big deal, I was sure I was going to be mugged on the street."

Elise, now in her early twenties, talked about how every gift from her Aunt Lydia is memorable and how noticeable her aunt's care in choosing and presenting them is: "Aunt Lydia doesn't give birthday presents. Instead, she gives really amazing Christmas presents and wraps them exquisitely. I remember in first grade she gave me some velvet knickers, made out of the most beautiful material. I just remember being told how nice the material was and knowing they were from New York City and the store where they were bought. I remember wearing them to first grade and thinking, 'Wow, I'm in velvet knickers. I'm the best-dressed kid here.' She'll get you a little necklace, but it will be from Tiffany. It's not like any of the stuff is pretentious, it just always has a flair to it, like the earrings that she bought me in Italy, or the gift from Morocco, or the bracelet from New Mexico."

Many aunties told us that the ideal present was not something they dreamed up, but the thing that the child just "absolutely had to have" but that their parents "absolutely were not going to buy." Wendy recalls her niece agonizing over the absence of a particular doll in her life: "She was in this little circle of friends and they all had these dolls and lots of the items that went with them. And this was very much something Erin wanted, but her parents both said that another doll was the last thing she needed. She told me that if I could give that doll to her, it could be her birthday and her Christmas presents forever.

I didn't have to buy her any clothes. Now on special occasions, I buy her things from the catalog of gifts that go with the doll." She added dryly, "Now Erin is able to play in her play group without further embarrassment. I believe the doll is also well supplied."

When we asked whether that felt as if she was spoiling her niece, Wendy replied, "Yes, it was indulgent, and I was happy to do it. And that's how I enrich her life. I don't mean just getting the doll, I mean that she is able to ask for it, able to have that kind of wish. You know how when you're a child and really want something—you have the idea that if only there was a fairy godmother, if only there was some kind of magic you could work, that you could have the thing you most wanted. What I think is really good in the auntie relationship is that you can satisfy that wish when the parents are providing all the practical things."

We wondered about the issue of getting in between the child and the parents on these kinds of issues. Do we run the risk of parental resentment if we buy a gift the parents refuse to buy? Obviously, we need to respect the parents' wishes with respect to the child's safety—a bowie knife or a dart set are not appropriate gifts for a small child, no matter how much they want them! We also have to respect parents' need for sanity—buying drums for a small child is just too cruel a thing to do to a parent. But Wendy thought that Erin's mother was glad Wendy bought the doll: "In a way I think it let her stick to her guns, so to speak, about what was necessary for the child, while still not having to say later, 'I feel bad that I didn't do it.' The parents get to maintain their point of view and the children get what they want. I feel good too. So everybody wins."

Perhaps some might think that we give children the wrong message by showing our love through material goods. But what became clear in our interviews was that gifts represent something more to a child than the physical object; they give the broad message that wishes and dreams can be fulfilled in life. It is worthwhile to pay attention to a child to determine what she or he wants and values more than anything else.

These aims are not fulfilled only by elaborate gifts. Carole, now in the book business, found that her Aunt Betty supported her love of books every year at Christmas. "What I most remember about her was that she caught on to my love of reading at a very young age. The one thing that I would most look forward to at Christmas every year was receiving a really nice hardcover book from her, like *Little Women* or *King of the Wind.* Every year I could always count on it, and I would save it and open it as one of my last gifts because I knew what it was. I would always have it read before my Christmas vacation was over. To this day, my nicest assortment of good children's books came from my Aunt Betty."

When we commented on her career in the book business, Carole replied: "I have thought about that a lot. Whenever I pack up my books, I look at the children's books that I have and think, 'Aunt Betty gave me this.' My mother did sign me up for a book club, but she never bought me books at Christmas. That was saved for Aunt Betty. I would always write her a note saying, 'You may think I would get tired of getting books, but you are the only one who gives them to me. I would be happy to get one every year.' I lived in fear that Aunt Betty would suddenly decide that she had given me too many books and would give me something else, but she never did. She always came through."

While the excitement of finding or receiving the perfect gift is gratifying, aunties do not always need to provide the ideal present to show their love. We are not always on target when we choose gifts for children, even those we know well. Rose talked about her clothing gift to her nephew, Vincent, who is five: "He was all excited to get his present. I gave it to him and he ripped it open. It was clothes. He practically threw them on the ground and went on to the next thing. You should have seen the look on his face."

Rose's sister, Marilou, responded, "I felt bad. The funny thing is, the next night he asked me what Aunt Rose and Uncle Brad got him for his birthday. I said, 'Remember? You opened it up in front of the restaurant—the clothes.' Then I reread him the card that Rose gave him. What she had written him was really sweet and he really liked it. He ended up putting it on top of the TV, where it still is." Even at that young age, what was important for Vincent was what his aunt had said to him in the card. The message made him feel important and loved.

The time taken to support these little people as they are growing, the recognition that they are individuals whose desires deserve to be recognized, are cornerstones to their growth into satisfied, functioning adults capable of giving love and encouragement to others. When aunties give the perfect gift, it is very exciting, gratifying to both the giver and recipient. It sends the message loud and clear to children that they deserve what they desire. By being given what one wants in life, we are given a sense of the possible, a sense that life really can offer what we hope to find. We cannot hear that message too much as a child or, for that matter, as adults. Aunties, with their generous hearts, their thoughtful gifts, and their celebration of a child's particular personality, help start us on a healthy path to adulthood.

Filling in the Gaps

Kids need our time, and lots of it. In fact, child development experts believe "unhurried time" with a few loving adults is as important to children as good health and a safe environment.

—HILLARY RODHAM CLINTON, *It Takes a Village*

$\mathcal{P}$arents are usually busy, consumed with working and keeping the house clean and the groceries stocked, not to mention getting their kids to soccer practice, flute lessons, and the other dozen or so activities they may be involved in at the moment. They also have the unsavory task of keeping their children on the straight and narrow—making sure they do their homework, respect their elders, and not hurt themselves (or others). Conversely, children tend to have lots of time on their hands, and they need companionship, a need that parents cannot always fulfill.

That's why we have aunties, if we are lucky, to help fill in those gaps. When children are raised by busy parents or perhaps by a single parent focused on the basics such as putting food on the table, they may feel as if they have fallen through the cracks. As

Theresa, now thirty-eight, recognizes about her auntie, "My relationship with my parents puts my relationship with my aunt in high relief because my parents were running around after three kids trying to keep everything in order. Aunts are special because they don't have to do that."

As we discussed earlier, a perfect gift lets children know that their wishes are worth considering and they are worth getting to know as individuals. But time and attention serve similar functions, albeit more subtly. Spending time with children and giving them extra attention boost their self-confidence. Aimee, an only child, told us how much she valued the attention of her aunt after her parents divorced: "My family, obviously, wasn't really stable. My mom didn't have a whole lot of time to pay attention to me. I didn't have a brother or sister. Friends at that age, well, you know how little people are. All the girls I hung out with were awful. It was really nice to be watched from a distance by Aunt Beth and taken care of and known from that outside, yet intimately close, position. It felt really good to have her know what all my friends' names were, to watch movies with her. She knew me. She was the only person from my dad's family who saw my house and knew my mom. She spent time with me and knew my likes and dislikes. She gave me a sense of importance. That's why I enjoyed hanging out with her so much."

Many women told us, as they thought back to their childhoods, that there were many poignant moments that arose from their aunties' provision of adult companionship. Marie, the hairdresser, described how her Aunt Pauline would spend time wading in the creek with her. "On the weekends, Pauline and I used to go to a creek not so far from our house. We each had these rubber boots that came up to our knees, and we would go walking in the creek. We would look at the rocks and the bugs. I used to sleep over at her house a lot. We would get up around five in the morning and go to the beach and walk around."

Olivia, a writer, talked about how her aunt was always around in her childhood: "As I got a little older, seven or eight years old, when Aunt Anne would visit my grandfather, I would take the train by myself in the middle of the night to where he lived, which was very exciting. The mailman would pick me up at about three in the morning, put me in the back of his mail truck, and drive another hour to my grandpa's. It would be about six in the morning, and

Anne would be there.

"She just kind of took me under her wing. It wasn't a talking thing. She would do my hair. She would tell me a bedtime story—there was one story, and she always told it exactly the same way. I don't recall my parents ever sitting down and telling me a bedtime story."

Frequently, when we think back over our lives, we have memories that stand out clearly, scenes that stick with us. What seem like small moments when they occur stay in our heads, especially if they are accompanied by a strong emotion. We found that many people we spoke with had wonderful memories of being with their beloved aunties. Goody told us, "One of my favorite memories was driving cross-country with my Aunt Helen and Aunt Mary. We stopped at Yosemite, and there was a bonfire where you could sit around and sing at night. I think being around that group-sing is one of my favorite childhood memories. It was something that my mother wouldn't have done."

Memorable moments, moments that let us know that life is good, were also on the minds of the aunties we spoke with as they talked about spending time with their nieces and nephews. Carole loves to share stories about her nephew: "Malcolm is my sister's four-year-old. We went to a museum, where there is one of those nail beds where they cap each side of the nail and you can push your hand against them. The bed then shows the shape of your hand. Malcolm had learned that the state of Michigan, where I live, is shaped like a glove, and he can point to where I live on his hand. In the museum, he was pushing his hand against the nail bed and playing around with it. I was standing way off to the side just watching him. There were about ten people standing around, and all of a sudden I saw this lightbulb go off in his head. He took his right hand and pushed against the nails from the bottom, and suddenly, he had created the state of Michigan. He points to exactly where Ann Arbor would be and says to the table at large, 'This is where my Aunt Carole lives.' Of course, I got tears in my eyes right away, and no one else at the table was paying any attention to him. So I walked over, and he said, 'See, look, I push like this and there it is, it's Michigan.' It was one of the sweetest moments."

Laura, who grew up partly in the South and has moved back to her hometown in recent years, told us how her aunt "filled in" her life and how important she considers her role in the life of her nephew: "The thing that is so important about my job as an aunt, that parents probably can't do easily, is details. I really believe that to a child, love is in the details. Love is the attention to those small things, because to a child, these small things are big things. Parents have many priorities. They have to look at the big picture and ask—is the child getting enough nutrition or is there enough money to send him to college? They often forget about those little details, the things that I can pay attention to for my nephew Tyler and that my Aunt Aggie paid attention to for me.

"One of the things Aggie used to do was make pear preserves from a tree in her yard. I didn't like the lumps in the pear preserves, I liked only the juice, so Aggie would make a whole pint of pear preserve juice just for me. Aunt Aggie paid attention. She knew what my siblings and my favorite foods were, and she always had them. That was how she welcomed us. That's what I like to do for Tyler. It's the attention to the small things. Now he is into this funny card game, so I learned the card game. Parents have other priorities, whereas I can focus on what matters to him. That's what Aggie did for me that was just so important. There was never a moment in my entire life when I doubted her love. She was very crucial in my life.

"Also, there was this incredible sense of safety and security. When my siblings and I were at Aggie's house as children, we used to have to take a nap after lunch. I felt so secure there. She did not let us fend for ourselves. I think parents are often pushing kids to grow up. I remember my mother saying, 'You are nine years old, you're old enough to take the bus to choir practice by yourself now.' I remember being terrified of that. But Aggie was always watching out for us, always looking at us carefully, saying things like, 'Are you okay today?' or 'You seem tired, you need to go to bed early.' It wasn't 'You need to go to bed early because you are in the way,' but spoken out of unbelievable nurturing and care.

"Whatever mattered to us mattered to her. I had girl cousins my age, and we loved making mud pies. Aunt Aggie had a huge yard with a big old magnolia tree that had these wonderful roots that grew out of the ground, and we would make mud pies there. All through the year she saved the pans that were burned and the bent spoons and forks. She glued broken plates back together so that we had a whole box of utensils and china that we could serve up our mud

171

pies on—those kinds of details. Parents would just throw them away and not think about how those little things would matter to us. We just had such a wonderful time. She took such pleasure in our pleasure."

Michele, a homemaker and an auntie to a niece and nephew, talked about how important it was for her to keep her "cookie drawer" supplied at all times: "When my niece Amber and nephew Jay were younger, they had a paper route and would come by my house, sometimes once a week. They always looked for cookies in my cookie drawer. I have always had this open-door policy about my home, and they had a key and would come in. I could always tell if they had been there when I wasn't, because the cookies would be gone. If they came and there weren't any cookies, god forbid, I would hear about it. That was always sort of a joke. It's interesting, because my own kids only get cookies about once a week! But I made sure I had cookies for my niece and nephew all the time."

Robin has maintained an extensive album/scrapbook for each of her six nieces and nephews from the time they were born. "Each book is a different color and has their name engraved on the leather cover. The opening pages have their birth announcements, along with pictures of me holding them as newborns. There are literally hundreds of pictures of our 'dates' together over the years, family gatherings, and movie stubs from the Disney movies as children—the more romantic, adventure movies as they grew older. There are special stories they wrote as children, plays they performed at family gatherings, pictures they drew while visiting at my house, and notes and cards they wrote over the years.

"The children, on visits to my various apartments and homes over the years, have consistently wanted to look at the Aunt Robin albums. It's become a tangible reminder of the hundreds of experiences we've shared together in their growing up.

"My intention when I began each of these albums was to one day give them their particular album, for instance, on their wedding day, or when they first moved into an apartment of their own and began life as an adult. I find, however, that I am not ready to part with those albums quite yet. Now I am thinking they will simply remain at my home and be in my will one day!"

Linda not only colors her nieces and nephews lives, she also has learned how to take care of some details for parents too. She told us how she provided piano lessons for her goddaughter—and also took the burden of making sure she was practicing and using the lessons responsibly off the shoulders of the parents. As she recalled, "My goddaughter really wanted to take piano lessons, but her parents said to me, 'She is not ready,' 'She is too young,' 'She is not mature enough,' 'The piano needs tuning'—five thousand reasons why they weren't going to allow it, but none of them were the reasons they had given her. They told her they couldn't afford the lessons.

"My goddaughter is straightforward, so she said to me, 'Auntie Linda, I would really like to have piano lessons. Would you pay for them?' I said that if I was paying for them she would really have to practice and stick with it. I told her I would be very disappointed if I was paying a weekly fee and didn't get to hear what she was learning when I came over. Then I told her I would need to talk to her parents first.

"So here was the problem as I presented it to her parents: 'I don't want to say no to her, because I think piano lessons would be a wonderful thing for her. I am not going to do it if you don't want me to, but you told her it was just about the money. Obviously if she stops practicing then I will cut her off. I would make that very clear to her. I'm not going to waste my money; she is either in or she's out.'

"We have had some fits and starts with the piano lessons, and I have threatened to withhold my sponsorship because things were not going well. I have a relationship with her piano teacher because I pay her and talk to her about how it's going. That way the parents do not have to be the police. I wanted to take the parents out of the loop. Dealing directly with her teacher has been the better thing."

Not only does Linda fill in a gap for the child by taking responsibility for her progress and keeping current with the teacher, but she has taken some of the responsibility off the parents' shoulders. Ask any parent, and he or she will tell you that parenthood gives you plenty to do! We don't know of any parents who aren't grateful when an auntie, generous with her time (and sometimes her money), attends to some of the crucial details of a child's (and therefore a parent's) life.

A Different Perspective

There are two ways of spreading light:
to be the candle or the mirror that reflects it.

—EDITH WHARTON, *The Quotable Woman*

*A*unties not only offer alternative life paths for us to emulate as we grow older, but they also may offer a completely different set of attitudes and beliefs with which to face the world, and a different perspective on what is important in life. Michele, now forty-six, told us about little things she learned from her Aunt Eleanor, who lived in the Midwest: "After graduating from college, I spent some time with my aunt and uncle. I lived in her home and became familiar with her way of living and her ability to organize things. Her way of life was very low key. It was probably more 'country' than the kind of community where I was raised, where we were busy all the time. There was a lot going on where I grew up, and as a college student, it continued that way. When I went back to Aunt Eleanor's, things were much slower paced—with naps in the afternoon and planning each event with more deliberation. I learned from my Aunt Eleanor to plan parties at night before you went to sleep. After you had gone to bed, you could think about how you wanted your party to be. These are funny little memories that affected me."

Similarly, Leslie, a thirty-year-old account executive, who is soon to be an aunt for the first time, loved her exposure to her auntie's way of life: "My aunt and uncle and cousins live in the country, and I grew up in the suburbs. When I was a kid, going up to Nevada City to spend my summers with the 'country cousins' was so exciting. It was a total down-home experience. They lived on a farm in a shed that my uncle built. They had a kitchen outside the shed, a few feet away, where my aunt would do all the cooking and then carry the food down to the tables in the shed. My aunt had a huge garden and all their food was homegrown. They even had an outhouse. To a kid from the suburbs, this was *it.* I loved the clean air, the woods, all the stars at night, and, best of all, the bright-red dirt that got all over me and my clothes.

"Like everyone else in my family, my cousin reads all the time. When I visited her, I brought my books, and she would disappear to read every book that I brought. So I would hang out with my aunt. I thought it was really cool, because I would help pick the beans for dinner, collect the eggs, milk the goats and then put the milk in big refrigerated canisters. I was in seventh heaven.

"My aunt is very earthy, very close to the land. I got so much from her about connecting with the earth, being outdoors. She would take me camping, which I never did with my family. We would get dirty and take baths outside. It was great.

"Each of us has also spent time caring for other children in one way or another. Aunt Sharon now runs a nursery school, which my uncle built on the farm. As I grew up I did volunteer work with kids. We have a real connection with respect to looking after the welfare of children."

Aunt Sharon's informal lifestyle was very comforting to Leslie: "I remember one year we were all going to go to Nevada City for a country Christmas and have dinner in the shed. My aunt prepared this huge dinner. I was eating asparagus, and was trying to cut it—you know how it's always tough at the end. I'm cutting and cutting and trying to be proper, and she leaned over and whispered that it was okay to pick it up. She told me this great story about when she was going to marry my uncle, and was having a very prim lady luncheon with my grandmother, her future mother-in-law. My grandmother made this very nice luncheon for everyone to meet the new fiancée. My aunt popped a cherry tomato into her mouth, which exploded and shot my grandmother right in the eye. First my aunt was horrified, then she just had to laugh. I love that story. My uncle and aunt have been married for twenty-five years now."

Leslie's memories of her time with her auntie continue to make her feel more rooted, more centered. One can go home again, and Leslie tries to get there as often as she can: "I took my husband up there. I can't describe the feeling I had just driving up the driveway and smelling that smell and knowing I was back there. I thought, 'I need to spend more time here.' I feel comforted, back 'down-to-earth' when I am there visiting with my aunt."

Leslie's aunt gave her a sense of connection, and she taught her the importance of being close to the earth and of paying attention to children as they grow. Others told us how their aunties provided an example of a good relationship, an example that they did not necessarily have in their own homes. To the extent that we are exposed to other adult relationships growing up, whether by necessity or otherwise, we can learn flexibility, that there is more than one solution to a problem, more than our immediate family's patterns to guide our own lives and relationships. Gloria, now thirty-seven, told us, "My Auntie Eva has helped me very much in that she has been married to the same man for almost fifty years. My parents had a mean and ugly divorce. Her relationship with her husband has been a role model to me of what healthy marriages look like. That's really wonderful."

Just as Gloria was inspired by her aunt's commitment to her marriage, so Dale, a fifty-three-year-old arts and health volunteer, was moved by her aunt's example to become committed to her community. Dale talked about her Aunt Alta's gift in reaching out to others around her: "Alta is a nurturer. She helps people be comfortable with who they are. She was able to break away from the insular quality that characterizes most of my family. We are really quite shy people, while charitable, and tend to keep a low profile. Yet Auntie Alta, by just being herself and by having enormous drive and energy and intellect, made sure that she got out into the community to work hard for not just family or friends, but for community endeavors. She was really quite singular, and continues to be. Auntie Alta has really nurtured my relationship with the arts and with nonprofits that specialize in medical help for people who can't afford a certain kind of treatment or education. I do a lot of volunteer work. I do it in her spirit. It's what we share."

Some people have been affected by a single aunt, but some of us were lucky enough to experience the perspectives of several aunties. Goody's aunts gave her a kaleidoscopic view on the world, which she illustrated by describing how her own three children have interacted with those aunts and Goody's own parents: "My daughter Marya tells a great story about what it was like for her when developing her own religious beliefs.

"Marya recalls going to my Aunt Helen and asking her about what happens to us when we die. My Aunt Helen gave her the Catholic answer: 'If you are good, you go to heaven and you can be saved.' She then asked Aunt Mary, who believed in reincarnation. She says, 'We go on to our next life.' Then she enters my dad's studio where he is painting. My dad was a Zen Buddhist. He says, 'We're all one with the universe. We remain forever in this faith.' Then she goes to my mom, who is a total atheist, and she says, 'Nothing happens to you. It is the end, that's all there is to it, and that's final.' So she gets four totally different answers. Then she comes home where my husband and I tell her, 'You need to decide whatever you want.' We are trying not to impose anything on our children. It was always that way—with me, and then with my children, my parents and aunts gave a varying opinion on every possible thought you could ever have."

Clearly Goody learned to examine life's questions from many angles. Additionally, she felt that her attitude toward money and sharing resources was shaped by her aunts' generosity with her, both in the time they offered to her and also in their financial help: "I have always been crazy about them, and you can't leave out the fact that they have helped me financially too. I didn't get a whole lot of help with my college education, but they all contributed a little. Then when I printed my first book they helped me come up with the money. I paid them back. I opened a coffee house with the money I made off my first book. When I opened a hotel, they helped me with that. To me, one of the most important things anybody can do is pass on an inheritance when other people have ideas, and when they have something about which they are passionate."

Goody's coffee house is a Portland institution, open for eighteen years, and her hotel has been open for eleven years. She gives her aunts credit for that:

"I have been able to turn the money they gave me into something, in both cases, that has made Oregon a better state, Portland a better city. A lot of people's lives have been enriched through my aunts' generosity. I have a pretty different attitude about passing money onto my children. I want to help them do the things they want to do now, instead of holding it back. I learned that from my aunts."

Eliza, now a corporate lawyer and writer, said her three aunts, who all were career women, unlike her homemaker mother, had a tremendous influence on her choice to follow a career and maintain an independent lifestyle. But she also emphasized that their priorities and approaches to life, all very different from one another's, affected her deeply. "They are all so different. Aunt Margaret was more of the matriarch, as the oldest daughter. She was funny and almost outrageous. She always said what she thought and could be irritating because she would always give her opinion on what you should be doing at any given time. She was the real supporter of my brother David, who became an artist. She had an intense interest in art in terms of being a painter and also in terms of loving art, so the two of them took art lessons for many years together. Jean, my mother's twin sister, is the quietest, the still water that runs deep. She is the one whom, if you had something bad happen, you could always go to because she would comfort you.

"Aunt Clara seems the most southern of the three. She's the spicy one, the kind of person who when she drives, leaves accidents in her wake because she drives just the way she wants to. She was the librarian at the local newspaper, which she called 'the morgue.' She is probably the most proper of the three. She can be very irritating, but very lovable too. Clara can cry at the drop of a hat and is a very giving person—very intelligent too. She has absorbed a lot from her job over the years. Back then the job was reading the whole paper and categorizing it each day; later it was developing computer systems, data banks, and all that. So she has the most interest in the outside world.

"All three of them are very artistic and have exquisite taste. They have different tastes but they have melded them together in this house where they live together that is quite beautiful. They have all collected different kinds of art, furniture, and rugs. So that house and their making a world of their own—one not just of genteel southern charm but also of artistic taste and temperament—has influenced me very much.

"They provided an example of how you could live. It had nothing to do with money you inherited, because all of them worked for their money, but with how you could look for things that were beautiful and put them together, devoting a part of your life, no matter how busy you were, to art. All three of them worked hard days, and would come home and cook dinner and take care of relatives. They made art more of a priority, I think. How they did all that I don't know. That's one of the best things about the auntie relationship. It's so safe but at the same time can be inspiring."

Who would think that a new point of view, an attitude different from what our parents have provided, could have so much power? Yet all of these individuals were enormously affected by their aunties' choices in life and by what their aunties found important. These women most likely have no idea how much they have influenced the children who have now grown into adults and incorporated their aunties' ideals and perspectives into their own lives. Our aunties' legacy is powerful, and we can be grateful for what those powerful women have passed on to succeeding generations.

Putting the Special into
Special Occasions

*The Thonga baby of South Africa is assured of a
special relationship with her father's sister, in whose
arms she is placed during her naming ceremony.*

—EVELYN BASSOFF, Ph.D., *Cherishing Our Daughters*

*M*any people we interviewed spoke of their
aunties' ability to make a big day even
more exciting, fun, or meaningful for them. We loved
hearing how different aunties made important events
stand out in a child's memory and the joy the aunties
experienced in making those occasions extra special.

A rite of passage that can sometimes be painful,
the high school prom was made memorable for Eliza
because her aunts sewed her prom dress for her: "I
could always lean on or look to my aunts. They
helped me make my dresses for all the dances. I remember for the prom we made a dress, and ten
minutes before my date came they were still sewing
me into the dress. I remember thinking, 'Did they
not put the zipper in on purpose, so I can't get out
of this?' When I went to the dance, they gave me this
little satin purse. I opened it to get my lipstick, and

inside was a ten-dollar bill with a note that said: 'Mad money in case you get mad at your date.' It was very dear. I had to fall asleep in the dress because I couldn't get out of it, and the next morning they were there like ladies-in-waiting to clip me out of this beautiful princess dress and ask about the prom."

Marie talked about her first menstruation and how it didn't remain a secret for long around her three aunties: "I was around fourteen when I got my period. I told my parents not to tell anybody. I didn't want anybody to know. But then I went over to my grandmother's house, which was a center of activity for all of us for a long time, and they were all standing around. I walked in and they all turned around and looked at me with these elated smiles on their faces, and I thought to myself, 'She told them.' They all came over to me and said the standard stuff like, 'Oh, she's a woman now.' They were gently teasing me, which is the way my family shows love for each other. I don't really remember how I felt at the time. I was probably a bit embarrassed, but now I have a fond memory of the moment—standing there, being stared at, knowing that everyone else knew, knowing there were no secrets. Now it makes me giggle when I think of it."

Francine, a thirty-six-year-old organizational development consultant, remembers her aunt commemorating her first crush on a boy: "During my adolescence, the first time I liked a boy, I said something to my aunt about it to initiate conversation. She ended up giving me a party. My other aunt had given me a doll for my fourteenth birthday, and that aunt gave me a birthday party. It was at Aunt Vida's home. She had just bought this big new house. They gave us the run of the place. They cooked and played music. We invited boys to the party, including my first boyfriend, who was a neighbor of my aunt. I think he was in ninth grade, an 'older man.' (I was in eighth grade.) It was okay with her, because she thought he was just the nicest boy in the world. That was a really big deal for me. It was a lot of fun."

One auntie was touched when her niece shared her "first kiss" experience with her. "When I picked her up one afternoon a year or so ago to bring her home to decorate the Christmas tree, she had just had her first kiss. She got in the car, and there was obviously something on her mind. We didn't talk about it for about forty minutes. Then she asked me if she could make a phone call from my house. I was beginning to understand that request as a signal, so

I asked her what was up, and she told me. Then the rest of the weekend she was in that giddy mood of not being able to think or talk about anybody but this guy. It was wonderful. I was able to share my own experience with my niece and tell her some of the things I wished I had learned early on about relationships, such as to enjoy the kiss and not to worry about what comes next. At the end of the weekend, as she got out of the car, she said, 'Thank you, you have been a great listener. My mother is the world's best psychologist, but she went to an all girls' Catholic school, and this is one thing she just doesn't understand.'"

Aunties take their job of enhancing special occasions seriously. Robin has tried to mark each of her nieces' and nephews' milestones with a special and very intentionally memorable celebration. "When my oldest niece turned twenty-one, I made a reservation at the Carnelian Room, which is a very posh and sophisticated restaurant in San Francisco. It has a breathtaking view and is the essence of 'old world San Francisco.' We took along the photo album chronicling her life and our 'dates' together and had a wonderfully warm, memory-filled evening complete with yet more pictures for the 'Aunt Robin album.' And that evening included the usual Aunt Robin rules: We can go anywhere you like, you can order anything you want to eat, you can wear anything you want, including Aunt Robin's pearls, and the evening can last as long as you'd like it to. We fell asleep that night talking into the wee hours about her upcoming wedding and when we would go shopping for outfits for her honeymoon in Hawaii!"

What could be more important than creating lovely memories with those you care about? Linda, whose auntie gave her pearls for her sixteenth birthday, learned firsthand how important her aunt's commemoration of that event was to her. She has since passed the gift on to her six (and counting) "special children": "There are these landmarks that are important to children that may not be important to grownups. The first day of school is really important. I call them and find out how it went and let them talk to me about it. I also think for little girls during those awkward years, Valentine's Day is very important. I might call them on Valentine's Day and find out how it went at school. And I always send all these children valentines.

"Getting mail is important. If I go away on vacation, I send postcards to everybody. I remember going to summer camp and how important mail was, so now I have purchased little functional items for summer camp and sent them to camp so they will have mail waiting for them when they get there. I also try to create special traditions with all my children. I might have them all over to carve pumpkins or to trim the Christmas tree together. My Jewish godchildren especially love to trim the Christmas tree because they don't get to do that at home. I really like those kinds of things. As they get older I am hoping I will get to take all of them somewhere."

Rituals of any sort, minor or more elaborate, create memories and cement relationships. We have heard of many rituals that aunties have developed for their nieces and nephews—Linda's pumpkin carving parties and Christmas tree parties, annual visits, even the type of gift a child might receive every year. These are what children cherish and keep with them, perhaps passing them on to the children in their lives. If we were lucky to have aunties who took the trouble to create or pass on a tradition, isn't that what we remember?

Rituals do not have to be elaborate, but their value is immeasurable, as pointed out by Dr. Pipher in *The Shelter of Each Other:* "[R]ituals connect family to each other, to extended family, to family friends and to the community." She goes on to suggest some rituals: "Interviewing family can be a connecting ritual . . . A good connecting ritual is sending children for long visits with relatives . . . I know of one great-aunt who has visiting nephews and nieces help her build a trail on her wild North Carolina land. After they work with her all summer, she names that segment of the trail for them."[15]

These types of traditions keep individuals connected, and help build friendships between aunties and their nieces and nephews. The essence of friendship is give-and-take. Our auntie may be our first adult friend and, if we are lucky and foster the relationship, we can go on being friends for the rest of our lives. Of course, friendship needs to be earned, as voiced by Deborah's nephew in this story that Deborah, forty-six, told us: "We were in New York this summer, my sister, my mother, myself, and my nephews. My mother was upset at one point because one of the boys wasn't paying enough attention to her. My twelve-year-old nephew, Bradley, got wind of this somehow and said with great indignation, 'You have to work hard to earn a kid's attention.' I thought that was a pretty insightful statement. Then he looked me right in the eye and said, 'VeeVee works hard to earn our attention.' (VeeVee is what they call me.) So it's what they feel coming from me. I really felt recognized and appreciated by them."

Clearly, Deborah's nephews learned from her the importance of paying attention to friendship. One of the nephews even turned his birthday into a special occasion for his Auntie VeeVee, which she told us about: "My nephew was turning eight on his last birthday. His mom asked him what kind of a birthday party he wanted. He said, 'I want to see my Auntie VeeVee.' She said, 'That's a nice idea, but what about a birthday party?' He said, 'I can have a party anytime.' 'What about birthday presents from your friends?' 'They can give them to me some other time. On my birthday I want to go to Sacramento and see my Auntie VeeVee as a surprise.' So she thought, 'How do I honor this?'

"Eventually it was worked out that another sister was already going to come, so they could piggyback onto the trip. In that way they knew I would be home, but I wouldn't know that everyone was coming. When the door bell rang, I ran downstairs, looked out, and there was no one there. I thought, 'Hmmm, that's funny.' The two boys then jumped out yelling 'Surprise!' and I burst into tears. It turns out that on the drive to my house, Lisa said to the boys, 'We are getting close—how are you going to do the surprise?' And the little one said, 'I've got a great idea. We can raise our voices up really high and pretend we are selling Girl Scout cookies and ring the door bell.' The older brother said, 'Don't be ridiculous, she would recognize you immediately. She has her ways.' I was just totally amazed that he would want to surprise me and that that was what he wanted for his birthday. The whole thing was so touching. I loved it that they thought I 'had my ways.'

"I looked at them and said, 'Okay, you guys, do you know what I would say if I were walking along in a village in the Amazon and happened to see you? Do you know what I would say?' The little guy was looking at me really seriously, trying to imagine that, and he asked, 'What?' And I said, 'What are *you* doing here?' And he said, 'You would recognize me anyplace in the whole world?' I said, 'I would recognize you anywhere in the world, even as a surprise.' I thought this was a way to help his understanding of what our bond really is. In any place, in any circumstance, I would 'know' that child."

Of course VeeVee would know that child, and

undoubtedly, he will always know his Aunt VeeVee. Children grow quickly and the more effort we put into creating memories for them now, the more likely we will be included in their lives as they get older. Ritual and special occasions are the glue that hold these relationships together forever.

Adventure with Aunties

Every generation must go further than the last or
what's the use in it?

—MERIDEL LE SUEUR, *Salute to Spring*

*A*unties can provide a different perspective, a listening ear, friendship, fun—the list goes on. They also provide adventures. Aunties not only teach us about new things, they frequently show them to us as well. Elise, in her early twenties, told us about her Aunt Lydia, who has been Elise's mother's best friend since they were four years old: "Aunt Lydia is very 'New York City.' Each one of my siblings and I got to go stay with her for a time by ourselves in New York. When you go there she takes you to the best Broadway shows, getting the best seats she can find. She takes you to the ice cream parlor that all the theater people go to afterward. She takes you to Greenwich Village and Soho and buys crazy sunglasses with you. She takes you to the Metropolitan Opera. She takes you to the best deli and shows you where to get the best fruit—things like that.

"I was nine or ten when I went on my first trip to New York. It was really cool. Aunt Lydia knew the city so well, and she tried to show me as much of it as she could. I got to go with her to work and to take a train, because she worked in Connecticut for a while. I saw what she did and the people she worked with. We went through Grand Central Station. I got a glimpse of what it would be like to work in New York City."

Adventure includes small excitements as well, as Elise illustrated: "When she visits me in San Diego we have other adventures. The Coronado Hotel is one of the nicest hotels in San Diego, and every Christmas they have this huge Christmas tree. Going to look at that is something we do—little special things."

Mimi, a thirty-eight-year-old editor, and her nephew invented their own adventure when they went "octopus hunting": "My nephew, Ben, who's now twelve, lives in Maine and I live in California, so I don't get to see him as often as I'd like. One summer when he was visiting with my sister and brother-in-law, we all spent the day at the beach. Ben and I ended up spending hours together, which was wonderful. He's always been a really goofy kid and easy to have fun with. I had him in my arms and I was wading out into the bay. The water at the beach is really shallow, so you can wade out for a long time. He suddenly got it into his head that we were hunting for octopuses. We started running around in the water chasing these imaginary creatures and yelling and laughing. We got soaked and covered with sand and hoarse from laughing so hard. But it really did feel like we'd gone on an odyssey together—an octopus-hunting odyssey, that is! We grew a lot closer that day because we realized that we could both be perfectly insane."

Rosalyn told us about the adventures she has developed with her niece: "We have our own traditions and rituals. For example, for her birthday every year I give her a trip. We take a week in the summer and we have had some of the most incredible vacations I have ever taken. Our favorite one is always the last one we took. Last year we went to the Sylvia Beach Hotel on the coast of Oregon, where each room is designed with a particular author in mind. It's the second time we have been there. She really understands and loves the place. As she says, when she's at home she suffers from the 'CTW syndrome,' which is the 'change the world syndrome.' I share those feelings with her. But when she gets up to the hotel, she understands how many people there are who think like we do and that it's not ours to do alone.

"This last vacation we took the overnight train

up from Los Angeles, at her suggestion. It was absolutely wonderful. I have found over the last few years that I really enjoy taking public transportation with her because it allows us to talk more than when I am driving. Our tradition started when she was about five and we went to Sea World for the weekend together.

"The year before last we went up to Vancouver, Victoria, and Whistler, and that was magical. It was her first time out of the country, and because of the way the world is now, we had to get written permission from her parents. She got questioned at the border, which helped make it an exciting and exotic trip. We sometimes help decorate floats for the Rose Bowl parade. We go to Pasadena and work on a float or go up the night before and look at the floats and then get up early and go back to the parade. We really have had some wonderful vacations and exclusive times together."

Karen told us about her adventure with her best friend, Pat, and Pat's daughter, Lauren: "When I graduated from law school, it coincided with my dad's seventieth birthday. There was going to be a big family party in France with lots of his friends, for a week. Then my parents and some young friends of theirs, two young women who worked for my dad, were going to go on a safari in Africa. I came home during this time and met with these two women. They said that between the birthday party and the safari, they were going to climb Mt. Kilimanjaro. They knew I was going through a divorce and that my life was kind of a mess and said I should go with them. Well, I had never done anything like that. But I had these two round-trip tickets to anyplace in the world from earning frequent-flyer miles.

"I thought I couldn't do that without my best friend, Pat, who is a great outdoors woman. So I called her up and I said, 'I want to give you a graduation present, because I couldn't have done law school without you. I want to give you one of these tickets and I want you to come to Africa.' She said she couldn't possibly do the trip without her daughter, Lauren. So Lauren and Pat both came to France for a week for my family's party, which was a turning point in our relationship. We became even closer.

"Then we went to Africa together with these two other girlfriends and climbed Mt. Kilimanjaro. It was an intense bonding experience. Lauren really became a grownup, one of us, on that trip. It was a turning point for me in that I saw she was seventeen and not a little girl anymore. We really were equals.

Actually she was not my equal—she was much stronger and more capable of the climb than I was. It wasn't at all like Lauren was just Pat's daughter anymore. We just were five friends."

When we asked Lauren about the trip, she said, "It was really an amazing experience. I had never been over there. It was so physically challenging, the biggest physical challenge that I had ever met. Having this group of women to do it with was really powerful. That was probably the first time that I had that kind of a bond with women and felt like we were comrades. It was different from friendships that I have had in terms of how much I could trust them and the support we gave each other during the trip. Also, I got to know Karen's family on the trip and I was welcomed into it."

Big or small, whatever the adventure, we find ourselves becoming closer to those with whom we experience it. Adventures are exhilarating, freeing, fun. We focus on the moment, and stretch ourselves to incorporate unfamiliar sights and face imagined or real fears. The danger of chasing octopuses, the excitement of seeing a new city, the joy of meeting a challenge heightens the experience, and intensifies the connection with our fellow adventurers.

Auntie Mommas

*I looked on child rearing not only as a work of love
and duty but as a profession that was fully as
interesting and challenging as any honorable
profession in the world and one that demanded
the best that I could bring to it.*

—ROSE KENNEDY, *The Quotable Woman*

unts always seem willing to step in and provide some extra attention when their nieces and nephews, or their parents, need them to do so. But there is a particular category of aunties, those miraculous women who take over the parenting of children whose parents have died or are no longer able to care for them.

Wendy's mother died when she was three years old, and she lived with a great-aunt, her mother's aunt: "My father was twenty-one when my mother died. I think he was pretty much at a loss with what to do with a little three-year-old girl, and I actually remember being taken around to visit various relatives, and he would ask if I could stay with them. If they said no, afterwards he would tell me to talk more, so I thought it was my fault. It was this really traumatic experience.

"When my Aunt Fern agreed to take care of me, it was wonderful. I lived with my aunt and uncle in Virginia when I was between about three and nine years old. My father disappeared for a while, then remarried and came back to get me to reintegrate me into his family. When my father took me back I was just an incorrigible runaway. I always tried to get back to my Aunt Fern."

When we asked Wendy about her relationship with her Aunt Fern, she said, "At the time, I did feel somewhat betrayed by her because she always called my father when I ran away to her. Now, as a parent, I have a different perspective. But I loved her because she took care of me. There had been all those scenes with relatives who didn't want me. She was a very sweet person. She was a wonderful housekeeper. She took care of her grandchildren. She was involved in the church. I think I got a lot of my interests from her. For me it was a real stable stretch of childhood that I can't even imagine having if I had been bouncing around with my father."

We also interviewed Francine, a thirty-six-year-old who took over the parenting of her sister's daughter: "Nicole is my oldest niece. She is twelve now, and she has lived with me since she was nine. Her biological father died last year, and her mom has a substance-abuse problem. So, I am also her parent these days. I did not have anything living in my house, except maybe mold, before she came to live with me. Initially I was going to take care of her for a month in the summer, because my sister wasn't taking good care of her. I wanted her to have a real summer experience doing things. That month has turned into four years this summer."

We asked Francine to explain the significance of being a parent as well as an aunt: "It has been an incredible experience. I am the oldest of my siblings and seem to be the only one who is not going to have any children, by choice and kind of not by choice. I am thirty-five now, and I just think it won't happen. I think that I am okay with that for the most part. And then having Nicole and being her parent, I realize how hard it is, so I am not sure if I would do it now. It just takes so much energy to parent. Also, I sometimes think that it's okay if I am not a biological parent, because I feel that this is what I am supposed to be doing, helping to raise her."

Francine's experience has made her feel that she has become a better person. It has also helped her see just how giving her friends can be: "Interestingly enough, most of my friends are single parents. I have always admired and honored what they did as single parents, but once I became one I had yet another level of esteem for them and an appreciation for what it really takes. They were there for me. That was an amazing thing. It brought out a sense of community.

"Right after Nicole changed schools, someone stole my car. She was going to a school that was not in our immediate area, so I had to drive her. I had two friends who immediately said, 'I can pick her up these days and get her to school, and this is what I can do the other two days.' I didn't even have to ask. One actually backtracked to get Nicole to school on her way to work. And these are single parents who have their own busy schedules.

"That in and of itself has made me a better person, because I felt that if people could extend themselves that much, there's a lot more that I could do too. When you have no children your choices are your own about how you spend your time, whereas when you have children, a lot of things are dictated for you. I saw that these people were willing to carve out another piece of their time to help us and realized that the least I could do was think more positively about how I could help too. Actually, every time I think about that it brings me to tears. It's just such an incredible thing to realize."

Francine also felt that her professional life, working in social services, has been enriched and improved by her experience of being a mother: "Being an auntie has taken on a different significance, because I also work on behalf of children and families in social services. I see my role as being this helping person, both professionally and in my personal life. I see myself augmenting the efforts of all these children's parents, be they my brothers and sisters or my friends. I see myself as part of a support system, because it is so hard to raise children. Taking care of Nicole has given me a new appreciation for what it takes to raise a child and just what single-parent families are going through to make ends meet and to do everything that you have to do. I feel like I have come to be where I am, with all of this, by design. Personally I've been enriched by having to raise a child, but it's also enriched my professional life and, I think, given me more compassion."

We asked Francine how she compared her role as an aunt to that as a parent, and she said: "Before taking Nicole in, I clearly saw my role as being the support person for my sister and the person who is apt to do the fun stuff. I was the first one to take her to Disneyland. I just wanted to expose her to different things and to explore things with her.

"I had her one night when she was about three. It was dark outside and we were on our way home. She saw something in the sky. She said, 'Look at the firecrackers,' but it was a star. It was just an amazing thing to see her first impression of a natural phenomenon. I remember saying in 1985 when she was born that her birth was the best thing that happened that year. It was our first experience of having a young child around and having her see things like that for the first time. That was my experience until I made that transition, which didn't come immediately, to saying 'I am her parent.' I saw myself as being the person who backed up her mom, another resource for her. Nicole could come stay for the weekend or I could pick her up and take her somewhere and then take her home. But that's exactly what happened then—she went home.

"It's tragic because my taking her means there is another family unit that is not what it could have or should have been. But it has given me the opportunity to parent, and I am very thankful and grateful for that. There really isn't any other experience that compares to it. I constantly try to think of it as a gift.

"A couple of years ago I had to do some internal work to become her parent. She needed something more from me. I needed to be her parent because she didn't have that. She needed to know, for instance, that somebody knows her, and knows when she looks a certain way, that she could be doing something that she shouldn't be. Things like that, that made her felt like she belonged. As the auntie, there lacked a certain intimacy still. So I had to get closer. I still see both roles, and sometimes they are very clear. Other times they are so fused there is no difference. She still does call me auntie. And she has called me auntie momma, and has even said momma. For the most part she calls me auntie."

What grace! Francine and Fern are both aunties who opened their hearts and homes up to a young child—they both saw a need and didn't hesitate to meet it. As Francine's example illustrates, the experience has not only fulfilled her, and filled out her humanity and compassion, but it has also given a child a safe place to grow. Perhaps women such as these were shown kindness and caring from aunties or other adults when they were growing, given a good example to follow when their turn to volunteer arose. Francine certainly had that experience as a child: "Here is what sticks out most in my mind. When my mom decided to move to California, it was sort of a spur-of-the-moment decision. She had five children, and she took the two youngest boys with her. I stayed with my Aunt Cora, my mom's youngest sister, and my sisters stayed with my grandmother. What I see as I look back is that they were very supportive of my mom. I think that we were apart for about six months. They took very good care of us. I was the oldest child, and my sisters would definitely say that everybody in my family always put me on a pedestal. I don't necessarily feel that way, but my sisters do. But I do have that with my aunt. I know that she has a lot of respect for me. If I ever want to go somewhere and feel good, nurtured, and pampered, that's where I go—to my aunt's. That's what she gives me, even today."

Hillary Rodham Clinton, in her book *It Takes a Village*, quotes psychologist Urie Bronfenbrenner as saying, "'The one most important thing kids need to help them survive in this world is someone who's crazy about them.'"[16] Most times, parents fill that bill. But if a parent is no longer around, or is so burdened that he or she cannot act on their love for a child, aunties many times take their place. They seem happy to do so. Imagine the relief of a child to be taken into a sane and safe home, knowing that they are loved. Think of the difference that such generosity makes in the attitude and beliefs of a child and the kind of adult she or he becomes. As we saw, the love and courage of Francine's aunt came full circle, and her generous example to Francine has indirectly contributed to Nicole's well-being. The auntie mommas, and aunties in general, who are willing to take time with a child, even to share in the grief and recovery of a child whose parents are gone or have lost their way, are the real heroes of that child's life. Most of us could take a little time and be heroes too. As Francine, and so many other aunties told us, their lives have been enriched by the effort.

I Remember
Auntie

I thought she was just the
most glamorous woman in the world.

—JILL

Life is the first gift, love is the second, and understanding the third.

—MARGE PIERCY, *The Quotable Woman*

Some of our fondest memories growing up are with our aunties—holiday dinners, trips together, shopping sprees, creating in the kitchen. In order to commemorate how we feel about our aunties, we asked the women we interviewed to share an image or perception they treasure most about their aunties:

"She wore Chanel No. 5. Whenever she had been in a room the perfume was there. For years after she passed away, every time I smelled it I would start crying."—Barbara

"We would go shopping together and I felt like everyone was looking at us. She was beautiful, composed, extravagant but not flashy. She was loud enough, but not too loud. She was the first of anyone in my family to graduate from college. After that, she went into the restaurant business. She had all these beautiful clothes. I loved it. I wanted to be like her. I wanted to dress like her. I just thought she was great and I totally looked up to her."—Aimee

"I remember a labyrinth of smells. There was the smell of Aggie's cedar chest, which she rarely opened. There was a different smell in her top drawer. There was the smell of her powder box and another smell when she got dressed up and put powder on her face. There was the general smell of her house, and there were always delicious smells coming from the kitchen. There was the smell of the sun on red clay. It is an amazing smell that I still smell sometimes. There was the smell of all the flowers that grew in her yard. Aggie loved flowers. Every morning she would go outside in her bathrobe and I would follow her. She made it seem perfectly acceptable to walk around outside in your bathrobe. She would make the rounds of all the trees and bushes and flowers, as though she was greeting each one. I remember her pulling the petals off one strange green flower, and holding it up for me to smell, and it smelled like bananas. I remember putting my face into her hands and smelling this incredible exotic fragrance. For a long time after she died, I kept a box she had given me with a scarf in it. I treasured it for years, not so much for the scarf, but because whenever I opened the box, it smelled like her. Eventually the fragrance faded, but I would love to smell it again."—Laura

"She told me that she wanted to die at home, so she wouldn't let me take her to the hospital. Auntie had a picture of my father that she told me she would give me when she felt her time was near, but wanted to keep until then. She gave me the picture when she turned sixty on May 2, saying 'I don't know how much longer I will be here.'"—Barbara

"When I think of Aunt Mimi, whom I'm named after, I think mostly of her putting on a Benny Goodman album and jitterbugging, scotch and soda in hand. She would laugh in a way that was almost a cackle, and her eyes would sparkle. I loved eating dinner at my grandmother's, where Aunt Mimi lived, because after dinner I knew the fun would begin in the living room. She was a good friend to all of us cousins."—Mimi

"She loves to have you come over and eat little snacks. She has tons of little candy bars in her refrigerator that she doesn't eat. She is one of those people who can have sugar all around and won't touch it. All the kids know that you can go to the refrigerator and she is really happy when you do. You'll sit down and she'll take out little candy bars and little pieces of cheese and she'll cut them up for you. As you are eating she will take your plate and sponge underneath it. Or she will sweep under you. It's not a joke. But it is hilarious."—Marie

"Even in the end, Anne, as sick as she was, wanted to go back home to Norway. She wasn't born there, but it was home. But after heavy-duty chemotherapy, she was weak. We met at an airport in New Jersey, flying from our different cities, and both our planes were late and we were trying to catch our plane to Norway. I was carrying all the luggage, and kind of hustling ahead of her, and she was trying to walk as quickly as she could. I turned around to see that she had fallen into the lap of a Hasidic Jew, who was just sitting there. My heart just sank and I ran back, and she said, 'This is a good omen, I fell in the lap of a religious man. We are going to have a wonderful trip!'"—Olivia

"You would never know that all of this hardship and these hurdles were placed in front of her because she kind of glides through. Physically she glides. She is a little lady and I picture her having a little magic wand. I have never said this before, but I always imagine that Tinkerbell sound, you know, the little bell going off, and things blooming and becoming 'more so' because of her. That's all in spite of the fact that her own life was never touched by magic. She made the magic."—Dale

"I thought she was just the most glamorous woman in the world. She would wear one of those short fur jackets. I suppose it was a mink. She came to the little country church that I belonged to, and when she walked in, it caused quite a stir. It was very unusual in a small rural country church to have someone walk in with fur on. I wanted to have long fingernails and have a fur just like her. I still remember that. I thought she was just beautiful."—Jill

"I think about her soft face, her wonderful smell, and, simply, comfort. I hope to be an aunt to my nieces just ten percent in that way. It is not a matter of being there all the time. It's about love and acceptance, I think."—Olivia

"They were role models for me from the very beginning, without even trying to be. One of the reasons I am in the career that I'm in is that my Aunt Jean, my mother's twin sister, was the clerk of the Federal District Court in Norfolk, so as I grew up she would take me into the office and I would meet the judges and other lawyers. I would attend trials and she would introduce me to the judges."—Eliza

"Connie was the kind of woman whose quiet forced others to reveal themselves. I picture her sitting at my parents' dinner parties, impeccably dressed and always gracious, a Deborah Kerr figure. The little curves at the ends of her mouth and the glint in her eye indicated that she was already 'in' on some inside joke. Her laughter made you feel as if you had accomplished something, and I can still hear it—even though she's been gone for over a dozen years—husky, full, sometimes narrowing into a chortle. As I saw her laughing, leaning toward my mother, smoke swirling around them, I thought being a grownup couldn't get much better than that."—Tamara

"I can't imagine life without them. I feel really fortunate. I feel as if my mannerisms are a result of all of them. Just in my own gestures, I can see things that are Pauline and Ruth and Nina and Fran in addition to my parents. I see photographs of myself sometimes and I think I look just like Nina and I'm not related to her. There is definitely a sense of being with these people for a long time." —*Marie*

"We both get up in the morning and we both have the same pace about things. It's the strangest thing. We get up and the first thing we do—we ended up telling each other this without knowing it before—is we go around to our various floral arrangements or plants and pinch buds that are gone and clip off things that don't belong, so that everything in our home environment is pretty and pristine and ready for someone to walk in and sit down."—Dale

"What I got from my Aunt Alice is how men and women interact, the husband-wife relationship. I never got to see that because my dad was too sick." —Elise

"When the women's liberation movement was beginning, we talked about that a lot, compared notes. She has always been much more liberal than other members of our family. We can still call and talk to each other about politics, things that maybe we wouldn't talk to other people about. We're kindred spirits in that way. We reinforce each other, I think."—Connie

"She always lived by herself. Which is my greatest fear in some ways. I guess I saw how you could live a really great life by yourself and enjoy it. She's really independent. She is very intellectual. All my aunts are really intelligent."—Elise

"You are talking about a strong black woman. A strong black woman way before her time. She was ahead of her time in everything. We often said it was the blessing of the Lord, he knew she was going to leave early. She just crammed it all into those years. There were some wonderful things my aunt did, and when I think of her courage, it gives me even more.

I know that she would have been so proud of some of the things that I have done. It was remembering her strength and courage that gave me the strength and courage to do them."—Barbara

"Aunt Mary was my mom's best friend and I remember the two of them laughing together. They showed me at a very early age how important it is to have women friends. Mary was a handsome woman and the mother of five boys. I always felt special around her because I was the only little girl in her world. She was my godmother and always gave me precious little gifts on birthdays and Christmas— perfume bottles, gold jewelry, antique doll beds. I still have most of her gifts today, forty years later."—Rita

"It was very clear then that this was going to be her last Christmas. I had gone to Minnesota not really knowing, but knowing in my gut that it probably was going to be. I had a ticket to go home and I kept extending and extending it. Finally, she said, 'How long are you going to stay?' and I said, 'Forever.' She looked at me with great love. We both knew that I was staying for the next step. Toward the last days of her life, she was kind of in and out of it. I remember at one point seeing her putting her hands together. I suspected that she wanted to pray, so I asked her and she said yes. So I had to dredge up some prayers from way back. You know, 'Yea, though I walk through the valley of the shadow of death.' I knew I missed a line in there and I kind of laughed with her. She was half there and with one foot in the other world, and I said, 'I know you know I messed up a line in there, Anne, but I am doing what I can.'"—Olivia

As these memories of aunties, both here and gone, suggest, aunties stay with us forever. Our values, our goals, our senses of humor, perhaps even our physical appearance and mannerisms, whatever our legacies from our aunties, will be carried on by us and perhaps passed on to a child in our lives who calls us "auntie." Although we may have to someday say goodbye to an auntie we love, her presence is always with us—in our memories and in the people we have become, as illustrated by the following poem:

The Photograph

For my great-aunt, Agnes McCurdy Crafton
(1888-1982)

In the photograph
the family has gathered
under the largest magnolia tree.

As I recall, some of them were leaving
(a second cousin and his wife and son)
and the rest of us have come out to
the driveway to say good-bye.

As I recall it was mid-morning.
My father is still in his bathrobe,
having slept late.
He is smiling but anxious to return
to his cup of coffee.

My mother and aunt are dressed for
a day of shopping in town.
My mother looks hurried and
wants to get on with it.

My brother, standing towards the back,
conspicuously tall,
is barefoot and not wearing a shirt.
I believe he was planning to spend
the day sailing.
He is looking towards the Bay.

My oldest cousin, recently married,
is standing with her arm around her husband.
The other cousins are laughing
as though something has just been said.

I am standing next to them
with my arms folded across my chest
not knowing what else to do with them.
I am smiling at the camera
ready for it to click.

In the center of the group
is my great-aunt.
She is too thin and is leaning
on the arm of my uncle.

We have all gathered around her
but, by her face, she is not aware of it,
Her smile has the gentle look of unknowing.

At our feet is an enormous shadow
where all our individual shadows have blended.
It has taken the strange shape of an animal,
a beast with many heads and wings and feet.

From the photograph, there is no way
of knowing which direction the animal
is moving—or if it is moving at all
or if it has stopped for a moment
to graze.

The shadow of my brother's head
is the animal's ear.
My uncle's shadow, slightly to the side,
is a long snout, foraging in the air
for the scent of enemies.

My second cousin and his wife
are part of a large wing that
the animal has folded back and under him.

My mother and father
are a kind of antler.
My cousins and I are part of his head.

And my great-aunt—
her shadow has disappeared altogether
somewhere near the center
in the heart of the beast.

—Laura Gilpin

Endnotes

1. Hillary Rodham Clinton, *It Takes a Village: And Other Lessons Children Teach Us* (New York: Simon and Schuster, 1996), 11.

2. Mary Pipher, Ph.D., *The Shelter of Each Other: Rebuilding Our Families* (New York: Ballantine, 1996), 151.

3. Evelyn Bassoff, Ph.D., *Cherishing Our Daughters: How Parents Can Raise Girls to Become Strong and Loving Women* (New York: Dutton, 1998), 53.

4. Clinton, op. cit., 96.

5. Joan K. Peters, *When Mothers Work: Loving Our Children Without Sacrificing Our Selves* (Reading, MA: Addison-Wesley, 1997), 137-38.

6. Ibid., 139.

7. Ibid., 162.

8. Bassoff, op. cit., 64-65.

9. Cited in Bassoff, op. cit., 63.

10. Pipher, op. cit., 21.

11. Bassoff, op. cit., 63.

12. Ibid.

13. Dorothy Corkille Briggs, *Your Child's Self-Esteem: Step-by-Step Guidelines for Raising Responsible, Productive, Happy Children* (New York: Doubleday, 1970), 45.

14. Bassoff, op. cit., 65.

15. Pipher, op. cit., 240-41.

16. Cited in Clinton, op. cit., 38.

About the Authors

TAMARA TRAEDER is a publisher, best-selling author, and intellectual property attorney. Tamara is the co-author (with Carmen Renee Berry) of *girlfriends: Invisible Bonds, Enduring Ties, The girlfriends Keepsake Book: The Story of Our Friendship,* and *girlfriends Talk About Men: Sharing Secrets for a Great Relationship.* She lives in Berkeley, California.

JULIENNE BENNETT is an editor and publisher. She is the co-editor (with Mimi Luebbermann) of *Where the Heart Is: A Celebration of Home.* She lives in Berkeley, California.

WILDCAT CANYON PRESS publishes books that embrace such subjects as friendship, spirituality, women's issues, and home and family, all with a focus on self-help and personal growth. Great care is taken to create books that inspire reflection and improve the quality of our lives. Our books invite sharing and are frequently given as gifts.

For a catalog of our publications, please write:

WILDCAT CANYON PRESS
2716 Ninth Street, Berkeley, California 94710
Phone: (510) 848-3600, Fax: (510) 848-1326
Circulus@aol.com
http://www.ReadersNdex.com/wildcatcanyon